Beyond Normal

A field guide to embrace adventure, explore the wilderness, and design an extraordinary life with kids

Heidi Dusek

Beyond Normal: A field guide to embrace adventure, explore the wilderness, and design an extraordinary life with kids

Copyright © 2022 by Heidi Dusek

ISBN: 978-1-950721-21-4

Harshman House Publishing
P. O. Box 82
Spring Valley, IL 61362

Praise for Beyond Normal

"Times have changed, but the way we look at success hasn't. Heidi flips the script and offers practical tips for designing a lifestyle that doesn't require you to commit 60 hours a week to your work. This book is an eye-opening guide for millennial parents who want to enjoy life along the way. Heidi also reinforces that growth doesn't happen unless you force yourself to be uncomfortable, which speaks to my adventure heart. Completely worth the time. Highly recommend!"

—Rachel Richards, author of *Money Honey* and
Passive Income Aggressive Retirement

"It's so easy to get bogged down in the day-to-day grind of life with kids that you lose sight of what it feels like to be adventurous and genuinely have fun. Heidi Dusek's wonderful field guide on designing an extraordinary life does the remarkable: it brings this life within reach and gives you practical ways to build a little more fun and adventure into your family's life."

—Brad Barrett, cohost and cofounder of the ChooseFI podcast

"As a hospice doctor, I have sat with those who waited until the end to reflect on their life. I can't help but wonder how many leave purpose and joy on the table for a rainy day instead of putting in the work in their younger years. *Beyond Normal* is a refreshing reminder to embrace the uncertain aspects of life as part of the journey. Heidi's adventurous spirit and guiding questions make this book both a joyful retreat and a great guide to designing an extraordinary life!"

—Jordan Grumet (Doc G), author of Taking Stock and
host of the Earn & Invest podcast

"Family adventures can be so alluring and intimidating at the same time. How do you accommodate all the different interests? I've long loved travel and adventure, but I've struggled to plan things for my family or fooled myself into thinking they need to be bigger than they do. I've learned so much from Heidi Dusek over the years about how to create simple, magical family adventures that bring families together. And in this book, Heidi lays out exactly the things we need to be thinking about to go beyond normal and plan regular adventures the whole family will love. If you crave more adventure in your life, you will love this book!

—Andy Storch, author of *Own Your Career Own Your Life*, founder and host of Talent Development Think Tank Community, Talent Development Hot Seat podcast, Own Your Career podcast, and My NFT Journey podcast

"Through vulnerability, insightful questions, and actionable steps, Heidi shares practical wisdom to generate adventure and joy for your family and most of all, for you. With clarity, honesty, and humor, she brings the reader so many gifts at once using stories from her life and learnings by experience. You won't wonder how to integrate the many unwrapped lessons into your own life, but rather enthusiastically try to figure out how many you might take on! And best of all, the path will be uniquely yours as it was for her and fueled with intention and courage. A must-read for anyone looking for permission to thrive and a foundational guide to getting there."

—Laurie E. Oswald, CEO of InteraWorks and founder of The Best Year Yet Foundation

I'd like to personally invite you to join *In the Arena: Family Adventure Community* at OrdinarySherpa.com/Arena or the free Ordinary Sherpa Group Facebook.com/groups/ordinarysherpa where you will find family adventure inspiration, support, and ideas.

You can connect with me personally on Instagram @ OrdinarySherpa. Thank you so much for your most precious resource: your time. I look forward to connecting and hearing about your adventures soon!

Be sure to sign up for instant access for all the adventure resources I include in this book!

Just visit: www.ordinarysherpa.com/beyondnormalbonus

Contents

Prologue

For many years, I was under the impression that you have fun during two "bookends" of life, first as a child and then again when you are retired. The middle section was supposed to be hard. This message made me believe I needed to enjoy life before the proverbial "settling down" period, when I'd work in my chosen career, commit to a life partner, and raise children; one in which I would be secure in my future and my kids would be secure on their paths. Yet even after a career, a husband, and kids were in place, I was still not ready to give up my adventurous life. I soon realized I needed to blaze a different kind of trail where few other families have traveled.

This guide will take you down our path. *Beyond Normal* offers research, stories, and tools to draw out the adventure in all of us. I share my journey of redefining success and venturing off the beaten path. Throughout this guide, you will find ways to assess your risk tolerance, stretch beyond your comfort zone, and experiment with tools to invite more adventure into your family.

As you will soon learn, adventure is more than summiting mountains and camping in a tent without running water. Adventure is means to try new experiences, face our fears, and seek joy like a seven-year-old. While some adventures take us on cross-country trips, camping off-grid or teaching our kids to ski, they also include the everyday adventures of exploring new places, trying new foods, and making play more prevalent than screens. Even with full-time jobs, three kids, and a dog, my husband and I continue to learn and recalibrate our definition of winning in life, work, and play. We keep adventure within our reach without going into debt or adding an extra hour in the day.

Every intention requires a mindset to thrive. The adventurous mindset has served me well. It is my compass into a world of discovery. As a field guide, this book is broken into three sections that align with Living Deeply, Exploring Bravely, and Playing

Wildly. In section one, Live Deeply establishes the foundations of adventure, defining joy and understanding the science behind why adventure is a powerful tool. The second section, Explore Bravely, dives into the emotional and economic factors that influence how we make decisions. The third section, Play Wildly, offers an actionable framework to begin implementing adventure with your family today acknowledging the challenges of a busy family life.

The Key Takeaways section at the end of each chapter highlights key points and reflective questions. In case you want to take a deeper dive into concepts within the book, the resource section offers several free downloads and additional learning opportunities.

Beyond Normal has limiting factors that I want to acknowledge. The guide is based on my learning and perspective, which are undoubtedly biased. I have the privilege to travel with my family, even if just to a local park, and feel safe. Practices to preserve the wilderness are principles we embrace, though not included in this book. The research around the impact of adventure and time spent outdoors continues to evolve. I am still learning. *Beyond Normal* was written to encourage "take what you need and leave behind what doesn't serve you" philosophy. My hope is you will find a few sparks that ignite adventures creating deeper connections with others resulting in timeless family memories.

Part 1: Live Deeply

Falling into Place

"At some point, we all fall apart. But hey, so do tacos, and we still love them!"
—Author Unknown

I always thought I was normal. I thought I did the same things everyone else did—that I had the same hopes and dreams. It seemed to me that we were all on a similar trail in life and just needed to hit the next mile marker of success. But when did *normal* become what we aspire to? I once thought success meant I had a big house and enough money in the bank; I'd be married to some good-looking, wealthy guy; we'd have a bunch of kids, and together we would travel, be involved in all aspects of life, grow old, and die happy. I curated the perfect plan to make sure I put the right pieces in place to achieve a successful life. I realized my perfectly curated plan was based on someone else's definition of success. It was what I thought I was supposed to say and what others expected me to want.

There are many spokes in the Wheel of Life. Many success metrics seem arbitrary and limited to a one-dimensional approach to life. If I want to take the epic trail ride with my bike, it's best if there is enough air in the tires, brakes are strong enough to stop when needed, and when the trail forks, I know which branch aligns with the experience I am willing to take. Wheels need more than one spoke to be strong; the same goes for the dimensions of our lives.

At age twenty-five, I had my first real episode of falling apart. I spent a considerable amount of time and money going to college to get a job I didn't love. I had just bought a house. I was in a serious relationship and thought everything was following the path I had intended—until I realized I wasn't sure I wanted to be on that path. The path to that comfortable life of success just didn't seem to fit me, and with each step forward, I felt like I was giving up more and more of myself in the process. It was like I was riding the paved bike path where it was safe but really wanted to be off adventuring on the single trek trail.

What We Want Out of Life

If I had to answer that question with one word, it would be *play*. I want to enjoy life, be goofy, and laugh often. I want to laugh until my cheeks hurt. I want to create magical memories with my kids and close friends and family that we talk about for decades. I don't want to care about what other people think, and I certainly would prefer not to follow the arbitrary "rules" of success.

Think of your seven-year-old self.

- Did you like yourself?
- What were you like?
- Where were you happiest?
- How did you enjoy a random Tuesday in the summer?
- What was the hardest part about being seven?
- How much of that seven-year-old is still alive in you today?

My seven-year-old self was a determined, free-spirited thinker. She was willing to be spontaneous, uncannily curious, and always up for an adventure. She was perfectly comfortable being alone for hours. She had a vivid imagination and would often write stories in her head. She loved an afternoon outside, when the sun was shining, and a slight breeze made the sheets ruffle on the clothesline. She'd bike the mile to her grandma and grandpa's house and be swept away into a magical world of creative play and folk stories with a side of unlimited treats.

She'd watch her three brothers go off on daring adventures, which she sometimes joined but was never quite coordinated enough to play at their level. Her limbs were longer and lankier than most seven-year-old girls' limbs. In fact, she was taller than most boys and would continue to be most of her life. She was fun. She didn't have a ton of friends but still felt included, even when she was off on her own. She simply enjoyed life. A version of that

4

seven-year-old has always been a part of me, but it was hard to see her at twenty-five.

I remember afternoons as a kid, playing school by myself in my lavender and mauve bedroom. The doll wardrobe my grandpa made me would transform into the teacher's desk. My imaginary students sat quietly on my bed. We'd practice math and writing. I wrote swirly letters and pretended to teach a writing language that was still foreign to me. I hadn't been exposed to formal cursive writing yet, but it felt fancy compared to printed words. I loved helping my imaginary students work through the challenges they'd face. I loved having cool things like the answer sheets; it all felt grown up and magical. I'd spend hours doing that all by myself in my room. If imaginary play had anything to do with my path, the days being a teacher to imaginary students in my bedroom certainly served me well. While I had exposure to teachers every day, teaching felt adventurous.

In the wake of 2020, while quarantined at home with my husband and kids, I felt that seven-year-old emerge. Simple adventures in our backyard became the highlights of my day. Then I remembered how similar activities had always been a source of therapy during the struggles of my life. This led me to launch the *Ordinary Sherpa* podcast to inspire families to connect through simple and authentic adventure experiences.

An Ordinary Sherpa

The intention for the podcast was to connect with other "ordinary" families who were craving adventure. A sherpa is often known as a guide, not the expert but perhaps someone a few steps ahead. The Sherpa tribe in Nepal are critical to the success of alpine climbers by helping them summit Mt. Everest. How can I help parents see the benefits of adventure without feeling like they need to climb Mt. Everest?

The podcast helps families by highlighting the journey not memorializing the summit. The research is clear: families who adventure are more resilient and have significantly healthier minds and bodies. In meeting with listeners, some need help to lighten the pack of responsibility they have been wearing for years.

I pose questions to my podcast listeners and challenge participants to determine how present the seven-year-old version of themselves are today. The results vary: some can't remember the seven-year-old version of themselves, and some are so strapped with responsibilities they don't feel the freedom to emulate a seven-year-old today, even for a few minutes.

According to Glennon Doyle and the research she reviewed in her book *Untamed,* significant conditioning begins to happen at age ten. We are taught to tame our personalities and fall in line with the roles and expectations of society. We are quietly groomed for educational pathways and careers. We slowly lose the vivacious energy of early ages. We quietly conform to the rules of life. It's not a direct telling or teaching, and for the record, I am not pointing fingers at parents, teachers, or any other sector. The purpose of this is quite the opposite. I want us to reacquaint with the younger versions of ourselves—a side that has likely been hushed for a couple of decades.

Discovering My Adventure Genes

There are two moments in life that gave me a taste of what was possible and turned on the adventure gene in my body. One was in fourth grade when my family took their first airplane ride to California to visit my great-aunt. Everything about that first experience seemed like a dream. I heard the ocean; I felt the continuous California sun in April; I tasted fancy food; I watched street performers. An overwhelming sense of wonder and curiosity showered my soul.

As a sixteen-year-old, I traveled across the world to be an exchange student in Germany, a bold awakening. Unlike my first airplane ride with my family, I was alone with a group of strangers en route to a similar experience. I knew no one. I came to realize how brave and confident I could be. Traveling alone compressed time and forced me to stop waiting for people to help me. Relationships developed in hours instead of days or weeks. I was thrust into responsibility and independence. If I wanted something, I needed to ask for it.

My time in Germany, living with a host family, opened up my world to different experiences. I rode a train for the first time—a novel form of transportation that, in my own town, only existed for cargo. My host family took me to historical landmarks I vaguely remembered learning about in school. School in Germany was a combination of less time in class, yet more formal and structured classes. I was given a window into a world where day-to-day life was a little uncomfortable and unfamiliar but surrounded by the kindest and most supportive people.

Taste of Freedom

The pleasure of my teenage years came from never feeling the pressure to be the best. I was able to experiment with all kinds of extracurriculars—from show choir and marching band to playing a different sport each season. I selected a class schedule that was intriguing to me. I knew others didn't have the same taste of freedom that I had.

I never felt pressured to go to college. I didn't really even feel nudged. I just knew I wanted something completely different from my small-town high school. In a rebel move, I joined the military and then didn't. Instead, I made a last-minute decision to go to college. I didn't feel the need to waste time figuring out my future career. I just decided to be a teacher.

I fast-tracked all the things to get to that point. I double-majored and double-minored, to keep my options open. I participated in any opportunity presented to me with no expectations of being good; I simply wanted to experience them. I didn't know it wasn't normal to graduate from college in less than four years.

At the end of my college years, I wanted a different student teaching experience. I enrolled in the Urban Education program, allowing me to complete my student teaching requirement in Chicago Public Schools. I went from living in communities between seven to ten thousand people to a city of nine million overnight.

I won't lie: I had a privilege lens and went to Chicago with an inner savior complex. I quickly realized my students didn't need saving. My first class included students from fourteen different countries, several refugees from the conflict in Bosnia. There were seven different languages spoken at home. The students in my class had much more depth than the boxes of their identity. I had some inner work to do. They inadvertently saved me and taught me so much about the richness of their lives. It was uncomfortable to be in the front of the class and realize you know less than your students. Teaching and learning became a two-way street.

Time to "Settle Down"

A year later, I got a teaching job at one of the wealthiest school districts in the country. I thought, *I made it*! I genuinely thought the hard part was over. It was what I had been working toward since I was seven years old.

At some point, society tells us it's time to "settle down." I never got the memo about what that actually meant, but I was pretty good at charades, so I played along. Each year, we'd celebrate teachers who dedicated twenty and thirty years to the same district. I accepted that was what success looked like.

I bought a professional wardrobe. I bought a townhouse with a garage and association fees. I did my own grocery shopping and pretended to cook meals. As a teacher, I took bathroom breaks at 10:15 a.m. and 2:15 p.m. because that's when I had a scheduled break without responsibilities. I took on athletic coaching jobs and nannied on weekends and holidays to make extra money.

My twenty-five-year-old self kept chasing whatever opportunity presented itself, working hard to please everyone, assuming my restlessness was just a phase. While my exterior maintained a happy-go-lucky stance, the adulting life started to feel constricting. Each phase felt a little stuffier than the one before, and I felt like I was slowly suffocating, which triggered The Unraveling. When life seemed tumultuous, I decided it must be the district I taught in, so I changed jobs. Yet something was still off.

Falling Apart

I heard that if you define success by using someone else's metrics, it triggers a mid-life crisis. I had succumbed to the fact that someone else's metric of success wasn't my definition of success, but I had no idea what my metric of success was. I had spent the previous fifteen years treating success like a destination. I was fortunate to speed up the timeline and had a quarter-life crisis at twenty-five. I wish I could tell you the one thing that caused The Unraveling, however it was a slow drip of someone else's dream life. I felt guilt for complaining about a privileged life I didn't really want; and anxiety for considering walking away from a life I spent so much time and money to create.

During The Unraveling phase, I simply began putting it all out on the table, like I was unpacking my suitcase just to see what all I had to work with. I wish I could tell you that with each item, it became clearer, and my pack got lighter. Nope. It was more of a "How the hell did that get in there?" moment. Imagine thinking you are grabbing a pair of underwear, and all you find are handguns. WTH! What kind of messed-up pack is this? This can't be mine! Who stole my underwear? I'd put it back in the bag and look for something else to do to take my mind off of it.

For me the length of The Unraveling phase was equivalent to the time it takes to do laundry after a long trip, a daunting, unending task that I avoid at all costs! I would do a little "unpacking" here and there, which ended up with years of work. By years, I mean decades because—let's face it—I'm still figuring it out. Some days, I'd fall apart gracefully, and other days, it looked more like straight-line winds were tearing things up.

The beautiful thing about falling apart at twenty-five was that it was a good time for a fresh start. This period is admirably referred to now as my year of "yes." I stopped waiting for people to invite me to things. I would just sign up, sometimes solo. When others knew I was game for anything, more opportunities landed in my lap. I gave myself permission to determine which experiences were one-time experiences and which ones I might want to try again. With each experience, I also wanted to be conscious of my feelings. Was I feeling angry, happy, sad, fearful, joyful, accepted, interested, disgusted? If I could name it, I could tame it.

My Year of Yes

During my year of "yes," I took a trip each month. On one of those trips, I spent a day at Katmai National Park with my parents, hanging out with grizzly bears. On another, I spent an afternoon on the set at Warner Brothers Studio in Los Angeles. I lost over twenty pounds in unhealthy ways. I made more money dog-sitting and nannying as part-time jobs than I made teaching full-time. I took trapeze lessons. I ran my first marathon, then continued to run marathons for several more years. I discovered friendships to hold for the long term and others to walk away from.

This might sound like an epic year, but if each of those adventures was a peak, I came slamming down into a valley deeper than where I started. I had spent so many years doing what I thought everyone expected me to do that I didn't even know who I was or what I expected from myself, let alone from others.

In October, I suffered a head injury at work. I was encouraged by the doctors to have someone with me throughout the night. I lived alone. It was the final straw. The accumulation of breaking up with a long-term boyfriend, emerging health issues, the weight of debt I took on to buy my townhouse, and the discovery of life between the hustle led me to make a change. At the end of that year, I resigned from my teaching job, put my townhouse up for sale, and moved— jobless—back to Wisconsin. It was through The Unraveling that I learned I had the grit to hustle and make life work, but I needed the space to fall in love with myself and enjoy life again. I couldn't keep escaping what I didn't like about my life. I needed a reset.

The first thing I left behind at twenty-five was a narcissistic boyfriend of almost five years. I chose a few adventurous friends who weren't intimidated by my weirdness. I began chipping away at the status symbols and leaned into things that allowed me to expand. I am slowly leaving pieces of that competitive achiever behind and picking up more pieces of self-awareness and well-being. It took getting lost a few times before I finally found the right trail.

Reframing Expectations

I eventually discovered that the unsettling aspects of my life had nothing to do with teaching. It had more to do with my obtuse definition of what I thought success meant. I needed a better scorecard to measure success. I became a complete geek, fascinated with various tools and frameworks that allowed me to see complex things in smaller, more relevant, and tangible ways.

I remembered the Year of Yes experiment and leaned into the concept that each experience could be a one-time experience and not require a life-long commitment. I listened much closer to how I felt, rather than what I thought. What became my checkpoint through The Unraveling and into the journey of life was this question: "Will this help me enjoy life?"

I welcomed the variety of different paths, trails, and terrain. I didn't mind the paved bike path some days; other days were prime for an epic ride. There were also things that I was noticing that really bothered me, and when I paused to ask, "How did I get here?" I couldn't trace it back to a moment or a thing. It was a series of unconscious decisions that likely contributed to a certain pattern of actions and habits that became the norm.

Resisting Society Norms

I began to notice that things others considered normal didn't sit well with me. One of those things that bothered me was the rise in specialization and competitive nature of youth sports at such a young age. As a coach of youth sports, I saw how *normal* it was for kids as young as ten begin to specialize and participate in travel league sports. I had the luxury of being a three-sport athlete in high school who never participated in a club or travel league. Yet I went on to compete as an NCAA D3 track and field athlete. Specializing in one sport and deciding what you were good at in fourth grade seemed like an unrealistic expectation going forward. I bookmarked this for a later date when I had my own kids and would revisit the idea of youth sports.

Likewise, it was *normal* to have kids as young as sixth grade begin tracking for their future career path. I made the decision at seven to become a teacher, at twenty-five, I was struggling with the decision after investing significant time and money. I didn't like the idea of funneling kids into a career track without ample time to explore their interests. In my opinion, learning is not a linear process.

In America, it is *normal* to work forty hours a week, yet earn just two weeks of vacation a year. The higher up the ladder you climbed in your career, the more hours you worked. Vacation consisted of leisure travel often defined by a work schedule with a specific start and end date. When did forty hours a week become the floor of expectation and not the ceiling for full-time employment? I saw colleagues wearing burned out, busy, and exhausted as badges of honor. Yet all these things made their way into life and were accepted norms. I didn't want to be *normal* anymore. I wanted to clear the cache and reset the cookies on my calibration of *normal*.

Course Correction

At thirty-five, a serious car accident while thirty weeks pregnant kicked off a tumultuous year. During my recovery, I nestled into my comfort zone, allowing status and spending to creep into our lifestyle. This time, I didn't need a full-out Unraveling to realize life felt more and more like work again. I heard the seven-year-old screaming from within. I simply listened and adjusted.

We don't have to completely fall apart to do a little course correcting. No one knows when you will need to course-correct except you, which is why this guide is not a technical plan; instead, it's designed to offer some healthy checkpoints and walk you through creating a loose itinerary for enjoying life.

I have spoken to hundreds of parents in their thirties and forties who have experienced a bit of The Unraveling. Through those conversations, combined with my own experiences, I have learned when we embrace The Unraveling and find that seven-year-old in us, we can begin to put the pieces together and figure out what to pack and what we can leave behind.

At no point in your life do you need to leave a piece of yourself behind unless you decide it's not serving you well. I would come to appreciate my quarter-life crisis. It was the best-worst year I ever had, and it led me on a journey to explore the unknown and find joy in so many ways.

Today, I am forty-two and proud to say that the seven-year-old girl is very present in my life. I have embraced the weirdness that I long for and appreciate that, as a family, we are willing to Explore Bravely, Play Wildly, and Live Deeply.

The Unraveling was self-induced and uncomfortable, and it helped me craft a new vision of a thriving life. It identified the parts and pieces that I wanted to leave behind and the pieces that fell into place. I hope this book will help you explore the pieces of your life, embrace what is possible, and give yourself permission to step outside your comfort zone. In the next chapter, we'll dive deeper into understanding our comfort zone.

Key Takeaways

Sometimes it takes a little falling apart to figure out which pieces weren't fitting right. Here are some pieces to check in your life:
- How much of that seven-year-old self is still alive in you today?
- What are some of your first adventure experiences?
- What are you choosing to say yes to?
- Which experiences are one-time experiences and which ones might you want to try again?
- Do you give yourself the space to reset, or do you escape the pressure and expectations of life?
- Do you wear burned out, busy, and exhausted as badges of honor?
- What does a *normal* day look like for you? Are you okay with that?

Beyond Comfort

*"Between stimulus and response there is a space. In
that space is our power to choose our response. In
our response lies our growth and our freedom."*
—Viktor Frankl

When is the last time you intentionally stepped outside your comfort zone? I began to notice my comfort zone was getting smaller as I got older. Let's face it, folks, I'm not twenty-five anymore. My body reminds me regularly. Things that were once easy are much harder today.

Last summer, I was in the Dakotas with my family, hiking, biking, and generally adventuring when my left knee started acting up. It was inflamed, sore, and unstable. I didn't want to let that get in the way of doing what our family set out to do. I grabbed a pair of trekking poles for our 1.5-mile Devil's Bathtub hike in Spearfish, South Dakota. I knew the hike would include some rocks and a bit of climbing over boulders.

As I stepped down about eighteen inches from a ledge, my left knee gave out, causing me to completely roll my right ankle. I felt defeated. I knew I needed a break and allowed my family to continue without me to the end of the trail, which is a delightful waterfall that doubles as a natural waterslide. I had to abstain from that adventure by choosing to miss the summit experience. I had major FOMO (Fear of Missing Out), but I knew continuing meant potentially making things worse for my body if I ignored the pain. It would make the rest of the vacation less desirable and recovery longer. In this case, the uncomfortable choice was to rest.

No Summit without a Journey

I could go all motivational and throw out a few inspirational quotes here, but I think I'll cut to the chase and say, "Growth isn't comfortable!" (*Yes, I am yelling.*) To design and experience the life you crave, you have to be willing to step outside your comfort zone. But it doesn't have to be torture either. I like to call the early stages *discomfortable*—the practice of doing something a little outside your comfort zone or on the margins of your comfort zone.

There are a couple of ways to enter into discomfortable. One is making the intentional choice to push your boundaries. It can be everything from talking to a stranger to trying a new food. If the scary thing is a sea you want to eventually swim in, discomfortable is the stage where you walk along the beach and dip your toes in rather than staying on the pier watching others.

It's cold! You can choose to stay in the water and let your body get used to it, or you can decide to get out. Discomfortable isn't meant to be an ice bath or cold therapy. It's meant to be one step closer to what is possible.

Every discomfortable experience is a little awkward the first time, however, there is usually enough to make you want to try it again. I have yet to meet someone who tried something for the first time and was an expert, and everything was as she imagined in her head. Why? Because learning is designed to be a series of experiences, trials and tribulations, peaks and valleys. Life is meant to be a journey, yet somehow we glorify the summit. We romanticize the summit without pain or struggle on the journey. The twenty-five-year-old version of myself thought I would be saved from suffering with a perfectly curated life plan. (*News flash, I followed the plan. The plan lied.*)

External Forces

Another way to enter into the world of discomfortable is when an outside force places an individual in an unexpected experience. A common external force in adventure is the weather, notorious for throwing a wrench in plans and making things less desirable. As long as we aren't in a prolonged state of danger, those moments of discomfort are temporary. Most experiences don't leave lasting pain in the process. Some examples of discomfortable might include giving a speech, admitting you were wrong, or walking to your car in the rain.

For me 2020 was discomfortable. There were many comforts of normal that I admired and craved, but there were also pieces of pre-COVID life that I was willing to leave behind. I spent 159 straight days with my kids before they were gone for an entire eight hours *(yes, I counted).* I watched my kids explore the depths of our woods, reminding me of the simple joys in life. I no longer drove ninety minutes to and from work each day. My kids snuck into my home office to lend hugs or leave inspiring notes throughout the day. I wore all my roles in life simultaneously. I had a backstage pass to my kids' learning, and saw the inner workings of their personality beyond the typical three hours a day. We ate at home, together. We explored locally. We made many different projects and challenged ourselves to try something new or different each day. 2020 showed me many silver linings and reminded me over and over again that I didn't want to go "back to normal."

The Science of the Comfort Zone

Our comfort zones correlate with the zone of proximity in educational theory. The zone of proximity implies the concepts you have mastered require little to no assistance. The further you are from mastery, the more assistance you will need. Likewise, our comfort zone, regardless of how big or small, includes things for which we don't need assistance. We have some level of mastery and experience. As we move to the margins of our comfort zone, we begin to experience fear. (We'll do a deep dive into fear in an upcoming chapter.)

Zone of dysregulation

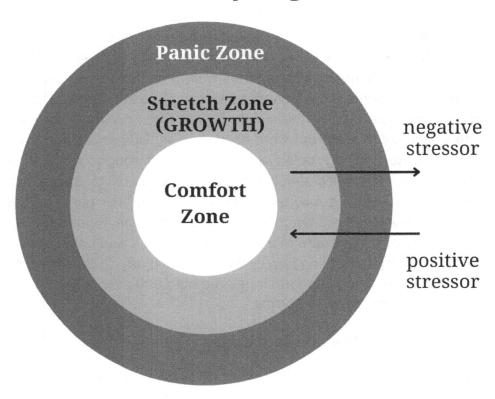

Imagine the zones of comfort as three circles with positive stressors and negative stressors, both having an influence on how we move through the zones.

To understand where the boundaries of these zones are, it's helpful to have a quick science lesson on the brain. The neurons in the parts of the brain that control feelings of anxiety and excitement fire similarly. The difference is how we label the stress response. There are positive stressors known as eustress and negative stressors known as distress. An example of a positive stressor might be giving a speech or going on a date; the stimuli are still successful in getting individuals out of their comfort zone, but they produce a positive stress response. Positive stress often motivates, is often perceived to be within our coping abilities, improves our performance, and aligns more with the underlying feeling of excitement. Whereas with negative stressors, such as a death, abuse, or separation, the stimuli also get individuals out of their comfort zone, but they go too far into the panic zone. The distress, or negative stressor stimuli, creates deeper anxiety or concern. The effects can be longer term and might feel outside the realm of our coping abilities.

Neuroscience and New Experiences

The second lesson today in brain science is the concept of neuroplasticity. According to Dr. Richie Davidson, a Neuroscientist from the University of Wisconsin-Madison, "Neuroplasticity is the brain's response to change and experiences."[1] Dr. Davidson became well known for studying the practices of monks compared to college students through meditation. The findings demonstrate that emotions, moods, and states are trainable skills. We have learned that we can change brain circuits.

Why do I share this? Because the boundaries of the comfort, stretch, and panic zones can change with experiences too. Much like with skill-building, with each small step toward fear, you might learn, "That wasn't so bad." Just for metaphor's sake, let's compare this comfort zone to your taste buds.

When I was a child, I was an extremely picky eater. I probably survived on the ten same foods. I ate a peanut butter and jelly sandwich for lunch. Every. Single. Day. Today, I eat a variety of foods. During a series of trying new foods, my brain realized the response I was assigning to certain foods was a mismatch from the actual experience. If tasting a new food was painful or bad, the brain would assign negative, maybe even longer-lasting trauma impact to new foods; I would likely still only eat the foods that were comfortable to me.

As you experience different things, your comfort zone will grow. As we practice stepping into the margins of our comfort zone and into our growth zone the emotions we assign to that experience will begin to change. Leaving the comfort zone is not always a linear experience. Nassim Taleb identified the concept of "antifragile systems," where growth happens through "volatility, randomness, disorder, and stressors," suggesting we purposefully practice antifragility so "we don't veer into the panic zone."[2]

We need a healthy dose of time spent in our comfort zone or our brains and bodies would be overstimulated. We regularly need to come back to our comfort zone to rejuvenate and process our experiences. If we stay in the growth zone, the new experiences become routine and boring, also known as hedonistic adaptation. Hedonistic adaptation often refers to a relative state of happiness despite major positive events of life changes. From a neuroscience perspective, our brains overstimulated hedonic pathways desensitize high levels of intense positive or negative feelings.[3] I like to think of hedonic adaptation as the plateau effect, when the effectiveness of a new experiences begins to decrease. Sustained growth also leads to burnout. We push the boundaries of discomfort and panic for too long, and the body and brain need time to rejuvenate. Sometimes what we have crafted as a *normal life* is already beyond our comfort zones.

Transitioning Back to Comfort

When I come back from vacation and transition back to daily life, I notice the tension between the comfort and stretch zones. My mind and body are still coming down from the vacation high, and I don't give enough time and space to rejuvenate before jumping into the intellectual activity of work. I have learned that I need my first day back from vacation to be mindless, catching up on work so my body and brain can recalibrate. For others, the front end of the vacation pushes them into a zone of discomfort, as home is the comfort zone. It is also the physiological response to burnout.

I had a conversation with a friend who really appreciates a predictable routine and for whom travel feels like a lot of work. His wife, on the other hand, craves an overly stimulating vacation experience. It was a classic example of identifying the stretch zones and comfort zones. In families and relationships, our zones of discomfort are not all the same. In this case, my friend's comfort zone was embedded in routine and the predictable nature of being in familiar surroundings.

Designing a travel experience for someone who appreciates routine is an indicator to me that for that person to be rejuvenated, the itinerary cannot be packed with surprises at every corner.

How can you build predictability into the experience? On the flip side, if another family member's comfort zone is in the snappy, high-energy, social experiences, that also needs to be recognized and built into the overall experience. Through a series of trial and error, we are better at identifying our margins of discomfort. We have learned four hours is the time limit for road trips or travel before we need a break. We also know that after two high-energy days, we need a down day to allow for unstructured exploration and independent time. We are then better at understanding the conditions of the experience.

We also have a tendency to aim for perfection. Memorable adventures are those when we experience both struggle and thriving moments together. These shared experiences provide a recipe for deeper connection among family members as well as long-lasting memories. Where will some family members thrive and others struggle?

Power of Shared Experiences

How many of you remember family road trips that stretched us as youngsters? We remember shared experiences, and much of our growth comes from periods of struggle and vulnerability. The power of a shared experience doesn't require the same perception of an experience. We recently visited White Sands National Park. While I was awestruck by the scenery and basking in the remarkable colors of the sky at sunset, my three kids were launching themselves off the top of the sand dunes seeing how far down they could slide. We had very different experiences; however, the shared experience was still spent together as a family.

A few years ago, I planned a five-day experience at Disney World in Florida. We are much more of a camping and nature family, so I knew we weren't going to simply make a *normal* family trip to Disney. I was pretty clear about what I wanted the experience to look like. I knew the insider tips. I created the schedule, planned for snacks and breaks, and it seemed like everything should be good. The night before our first day at Disney, I had a massive anxiety attack. I couldn't breathe or sleep. I am flexible and nimble. Structure and schedules feel suffocating.

When I plan our travels, I have all the details laid out with all the potential options. However, I don't care if we follow the plan; I just like knowing the options. I had been planning the trip and knew what to expect, but it felt like in order to have the best experience, we needed to follow the plan. If we didn't get there on time, it would throw the entire schedule off. I thought waiting in long lines for the rides would ruin the experience. Or missing the character we were hoping to see would be upsetting.

The good news was Disney was magical, and we loved it all, but we quickly realized our favorite part every day was coming back to the condo around lunch, taking a nap, and playing in the pool. What logically seemed like a waste of money when I was creating the schedule was actually where we all connected and were able to rejuvenate. Then in the late afternoon or evening, we could decide if we wanted to return to any rides or activities in the park. On day two, we accomplished everything we wanted to before noon. We had an unplanned down day on day three, which finally allowed me to settle into the flexible experience I was craving.

Identifying the Comfort Zone

There is growing research that shows travel and adventure that exposes individuals to new and uncomfortable experiences is good for their mental health. "Want to maximize your brain's neuroplasticity? A change of scenery wakes up your brain and takes it off autopilot. You have to think about small things when you're in an unfamiliar place, which is the point. Learning a few words of a different language, taking a walking tour, or even something as simple as trying a new food can get those neurons firing."[4] Even the anticipation and planning of an experience can release dopamine, a neurotransmitter responsible for helping individuals feel good.

Sometimes, it's easy to get influenced by outside forces. As much as I alluded to the magic of a down day, we still tend to jam-pack unbelievable amounts of adventure into our travel experiences. For a recent twelve-day RV trip, we crafted the general concept of a route and researched the activities and attractions available along the way. We didn't make many reservations at traditional campsites. We wanted to go with the flow and not feel like we had to reach a certain destination. However, I thought we might need a mid-trip break from camping and nature, so I booked an overpriced campsite with all the amenities thinking the kids would really appreciate a kid day. When we arrived, I knew it was not the style that best fit my husband and me. The campground was packed. Many RVs were outfitted with satellite dishes; dozens of golf carts and ATVs roamed the grounds; there were waterslides and mini-golf, along with a full schedule of activities. I thought the kids would be thrilled.

The kids eagerly got changed to go to the waterslide and explore all the fun things they saw when we drove in. The initial excitement waned quickly, and the kids confessed, "We really liked the campsite we had last night better." We just came off a free night of boondocking (camping in the wilderness without electricity or water hookups) at a creek with a swimming area, waterfalls, fishing, an epic sunset, and only a handful of other campers. I had fallen prey to letting someone else decide what our comfort zone was. We made the best of it and watched a movie and ate popcorn, took showers, and did a load of laundry. But there was no love lost when we left the next day.

I have learned to question the relevance of people who give travel advice, saying things like, "Your family is going to *love* it" if they don't really know our family. Our comfort zones are pretty broad, and we have experienced quite a bit in our life. It's difficult to prescribe for others what will stretch them without a close relationship. Rather than give advice, I try to share our experiences and a bit about what stretched us.

Hanging out in the comfort zone can do more harm than good. Rather than fearing the stretch zone, I encourage families to embrace the practice of going beyond their comfort zone each week. Recognizing opportunities to leave the comfort zone is not always easy. Being receptive to opportunities and challenging the status quo requires self-reflection and awareness. When you build the habit of noticing the opportunities, choosing which ones to say yes to, and taking the first step forward, you quickly see the rewards. Stacking these rewards, over time, you will realize that you are able to curb disappointments more easily and explore the depths of your potential.

"Great. Where do I start?"

[Cue adventure].

Key Takeaways

The practice of stepping out of your comfort zone does not need to be big and scary. These are some questions to identify the margins of discomfort in your life:

- Do you notice what excites you and scares you at the same time? It's probably a sign you need to take the next first step to get uncomfortable.
- When do you need to come back to comfort? Our brain will adapt to new experiences and lead to either overstimulation or desensitization.
- How can you build predictability into the experience?
- When designing adventures, what seems logical or a waste of money? Why? We sometimes think we have to stay in growth and discomfort for a meaningful experience. During our Disney trip, the illogical space in the schedule was actually where we all connected and were able to rejuvenate.
- How did you go beyond your comfort zone this week?
- Does the person offering travel advice know your family? Travel advice without a relationship might lead to a shallow and costly experience. I encourage listening to others' experiences then deciding whether it is a good fit for your family or an extension of tourism marketing.

Not Adventurous

"It is not the critic who counts; not the man who points out how the strong man stumbles, or where the doer of deeds could have done them better. The credit belongs to the man who is actually in the arena, whose face is marred by dust and sweat and blood; who strives valiantly; who errs, who comes short again and again, because there is no effort without error and shortcoming; but who does actually strive to do the deeds; who knows great enthusiasms, the great devotions; who spends himself in a worthy cause; who at the best knows in the end the triumph of high achievement, and who at the worst, if he fails, at least fails while daring greatly, so that his place shall never be with those cold and timid souls who neither know victory nor defeat."
—Teddy Roosevelt

Adventure implies a wild ride. Just for fun, when you think of adventure, what picture comes to mind? What do you see? Hear? Smell? Taste? Feel? We can pack quite a few thoughts and experiences into our minds pretty quickly.

Did you imagine a younger adult doing epic outdoor sports in the wilderness? It's *normal* to think that when you have kids, your adventure life is over.

Are you thinking of a time when you went to a nature preserve? The bugs swarmed your head; you misstepped, landing in mud, making your shoe soggy for the rest of the hike; a snake scurried across your path, scaring you from hiking that trail again. Is that what you are envisioning as an adventure? It's *normal* to think you must love the allure of the wilderness in order to be adventurous.

Are you watching a documentary of a person who completes epic adventures biking across the country? It's *normal* to think we need days, weeks, or months of time in order to experience a meaningful adventure.

Or are you thinking of those mountain climbers who post pictures at the summit of the highest peaks? Every time you see those pictures, you think, *They are badass adventurers!* It's *normal* to think adventure includes extreme sports or high-risk activities.

Limiting Beliefs

In my unsophisticated market assessment, I began to hear the phrase, "I'm not adventurous" or "I wish I were adventurous." When I learned how they see adventure, it was often a pretty epic summit or something outdoorsy that just didn't align with that person's creature comforts.

Our beliefs are the assumptions we hold to be true. Beliefs are built and reinforced over time based on relationships, experiences, and observing our surroundings. However, when we fail to examine our beliefs and bring them to the conscious level, we run the risk of basing decisions on false or inaccurate data.

There are many ways to self-select out of an opportunity, and the most widely used phrase begins with "I am not _____." You can fill in the blank with any trait (creative, a reader, a writer, handy, good with plants, strategic, tech-savvy—you name it). When I hear this phrase, it's the first indicator of a limiting belief. Somewhere in your life, you had an experience that reinforced this belief, causing it to become your truth. It usually comes as the result of comparing yourself to another person. If we dig into our limiting beliefs as an opportunity for curiosity, we can dig deeper and learn, "Why do I think that way?"

I have always said, "I am not a reader." I did just enough to get by in school. Reading just wasn't what we did in our house, and I could find a thousand other things to do rather than read. Over the years, I've been curious as people talk about books. I slowly began to add a book or two to my list. I joined a book club to add some accountability to read a book a month with the added social benefits.

In the last six months, I have independently read seventeen books, sometimes completing an entire fifteen-chapter nonfiction book in a weekend. At what point would I declare myself a reader? How do I define a reader? Is there a benchmark for "good enough" to eliminate that limiting belief? We'll discuss benchmarks of achievement in a later chapter. For this chapter, we are going to dive deeper into the limiting belief, "I am not adventurous," or even "I used to be adventurous," implying that you are too old or that your life stage is not ideal for adventure.

Definition of Adventure

According to *Miriam-Webster Dictionary*, the definition of *adventure* is
   a: an undertaking usually involving danger and unknown risks
   b: an exciting or remarkable experience

Ironically, the definition of *adventure* does not include any reference to the outdoors, yet most people immediately frame adventure into an unachievable outdoor experience. A standard coaching practice is maintaining an underlying belief that our thoughts control our feelings. If you want to change how you feel about something, you must change how you think about it. Instead of thinking adventure is hard, I am going to take you through a different way to think about it.

Western society has a love affair with perceived perfection, which prohibits many from signing up to simply fail for learning's sake. I decided to lighten the blow of potential failure by framing the opportunities with a mindset of adventure. Built into the mindset of adventure is an assumption of risks alongside exciting results or remarkable experiences. Significant research shows that adventure is a platform to help people learn about interpersonal relationships (with others) and intrapersonal relationships (with self). With each new experience, you learn something new about yourself, or you might connect with someone else on the journey.

Running in the Rain

During my falling apart at age twenty-five, I signed up to run my first marathon. I knew myself well enough to know that I wouldn't train on my own; I needed others to hold me accountable for my progress. I signed up with a charitable organization that had a system for supporting runners in accomplishing the adventure in exchange for runners raising money to support their mission.

While the initial reason for signing up was to complete a marathon, I quickly learned the interpersonal and intrapersonal growth that developed through the six months of training would forever change the trajectory of my life. I met other participants from all walks of life, with different running histories, ages, and careers. They helped me reframe my belief of "I'm not a runner" into "I run marathons."

During one particular training run, I remember the skies slowly shifted from overcast to sprinkling, and eventually, full-scale downpour. There were about five other female runners in my pace group, and we all were a little bit startled. I don't think any of us had willingly run in a rainstorm like that before. After the initial shock wore off and we were still running away from the trailhead, we shifted our mindset from disbelief and uncomfortable to playful and childlike. We shifted from steady strides to dodging puddles or splashing through them, from casual conversation to giggling loudly, and an occasional shriek of unexpected dousing when the tree branches swayed with the breeze. We were all a bit amused that the entire team was still trudging forward with the training run.

Eventually, the rain eased up, and we continued, drenched, muddy, filled with joy and a bit of disbelief that we were still running. The shared experience of running in the rain would create a new level of connection with my fellow teammates. I never forgot that experience, that connection, or that part of the journey in completing my first marathon.

Connecting through Struggle

Running in the rain was a powerful experience because it taught me so many things about life. There will be periods in your life that will be a downpour, and you might feel stuck and unprepared. You can choose to stop moving forward and potentially hide under a tree, or you can choose to keep taking steps forward, get muddy, attempt to dodge the puddles, and still enjoy the experience. I don't know many who willingly sign up to run in the rain. It's not a pleasant experience and has implications for the final results. I also know that once you finish a run in the rain, you can look back with a different level of confidence and pride. You did this.

To me, it's the equivalent of Teddy Roosevelt's Man in the Arena quotation above being *"marred by dust and sweat and blood."* This experience won't make sense to many others, but it will have a lasting impression on your life. Don't feel like it's your job to explain to others why you are embarking on this experience. You don't have to have it all figured out, and you are not responsible for their understanding.

Running in the rain also taught me about the importance of finding my tribe. The struggle we shared running in the rain led to deeper connections with my teammates. If I were running in the rain with five people who didn't have a vested interest in the adventure of running a marathon, we likely would have complained as we turned back to our cars seeking the comforts of a normal life.

Many people do not understand why I pay to run 26.2 miles or why I willingly run hundreds of miles leading up to my races. It just doesn't make sense to them. It's okay. It doesn't have to make sense. I don't need their permission to do something that stretches me. Regardless of the adventure you decide to take, there will always be others both ahead of you and behind you on this journey. You will know you have found your tribe when the ones ahead of you are reaching back with a willing hand, offering to help you out. Likewise, the ones behind you are pushing you forward and cheering you on. The tribe will bring you the energy and persistence you need to keep going when your stash is depleted. Having a tribe is a critical and underrated component when working through significant periods of stretch and struggle.

Purposeful Discomfort

I want to be explicit about something here. I know some of you might be thinking, *I don't want to run a marathon,* and my response is, "You don't have to." This section is not about adopting what I think adventure is or defining a list of adventures that are bucket list worthy. This is about bringing unconscious thoughts into active consciousness and being intentional about the life you want to experience. If we aren't intentional about experiencing purposeful discomfort, life will continue to exist in the drift state of daily comforts.

As a parent, I quickly noticed that the level of adventure I was willing to sign up for diminished rapidly. I had the initial mindset that *I would do everything in my power to keep my kids safe.* One of the reasons I felt compelled to write this book was to offer parents a guide for how to embrace adventures that feel uncomfortable or risky with our children.

We live in the bubble wrap era, and there are a million ways we can screw up our kids. Every time I learned something new, there was sudden fear or questioning, "Am I doing this right?" Over the years, I have learned that perfection is selfish and stifling. If I wanted a perfect life, it would mean depriving my kids of many opportunities disguised as safety and stability. If I waited for perfection to show up, I'd be inadvertently saying no to so many opportunities for authentic connection.

Risky Play

Adventure offers real developmental and health benefits. When kids experience risk, they begin their own process of self-discovery. Where is their comfort zone? Adventure allows them to test boundaries and build their self-confidence. They become familiar with their bodies in relation to the external environment, thus improving coordination, awareness, and adaptability. A key lesson for me was risky play—play that gets kids out of the upright position—is required for kids to develop their vestibular sense and coordination skills, making them safer in the long run. [5]

The vestibular sense is the sensory system located in the inner ear that contributes to balance, spatial awareness, and muscle tone. An underdeveloped vestibular sense affects many other systems. It can affect the eyes in reading and writing and affect our posture. Kids are neurologically and naturally drawn to movements that have them flipping upside down or spinning in circles, yet adults often prohibit those and reinforce upright positions from a narrative of safety.

I recognized my risk threshold as a parent was much higher than some of my peers, and it continues to get tested. A risk assessment in business is a process to identify potential hazards and analyze the severity of the outcome if the hazard occurs. I replicated this process when assessing risky play by comparing the severity of the potential outcome with the probability the outcome will happen. When considering adventure with kids, I look for the conditions to allow "just enough" risk to help them develop their skills while minimizing the severity of harm. Hiking on a trail in the woods has a much lower risk than hiking on top of a cliff along the ocean.

Assessing Risk

One summer, we took a long weekend trip to Ohio. We like to visit Major League Baseball stadiums and national parks, and when we can get both in one trip, we get really excited. We made plans to visit Cuyahoga National Park and were eager to bike the towpath and hike to all the waterfalls. I happen to have a nature crush on waterfalls. We checked out several waterfalls and spent hours biking, when it started to sprinkle. We had three waterfalls left to explore and decided it was worth continuing the journey.

While we were driving to the next trailhead, our youngest fell asleep. I hiked to a waterfall with the older two while my husband stayed back with our little guy in the car. The trail was a bit tricky with some pretty big rocks, and runoff ditches had formed throughout the gravel trail. The damp mist made the larger rocks slick, adding an extra layer of risk, requiring more caution.

My daughter took a spill on the trail about halfway to the waterfall—a fall that resulted in a scrape and dirty hands. To her, the sight of blood, dirt, and wet clothes was a recipe for drama. After some creative parenting and spontaneous psychology, we were able to continue to the waterfall. The sights, sounds, and exploration at the waterfall offered a calming scene, which knocked the recent experience out of our zone of consciousness. We cascaded into the exploratory world, and after some time, hiked back to the car.

As my daughter climbed into the back seat, she caught a glimpse of her knee and was reminded of her fall, the scrape and blood still visible. She simply said, "Hmm, it doesn't hurt anymore.

These are a sign of my memories now!" The once traumatic and dramatic experience of falling on the trail would now have a different memory attached to it—a memory of overcoming.

There are two other risk tolerance experiences that come to mind. Once, we took an intense trail along the southern Oregon coast where there were elements of the trail that traversed narrow cliffs, and a fall could lead to the rocky ocean below. A deadly incident was possible. That alone triggered my anxiety enough to believe the risk was high. I allowed my fear of danger to be the loudest voice, and in this instance, my husband was on board. We didn't complete the trail but returned to our comfort zone.

While camping cliffside on the north shore of the Big Island of Hawaii, there was a similar but different experience. My daughter had visions of us rolling off the cliff, and her anxiety was off the charts. Through the support and encouragement of her family, she wrote a different internal narrative about the risk, which included a low probability of us falling off the cliff. As we were preparing to leave that campsite, my oldest son asked if we could take the ladder and ropes that were available to climb down the cliff to get closer to the rocky shore. I knew I wasn't going to be able to do that and support the kids in the process. I asked my husband how he felt about it. He tested the ladder and the route so he could determine the likelihood of harm and decided he was willing to guide them. All three kids took the ladder down a cliff to traverse the rocky shoreline. Their stretch zone was my panic zone—another lesson in overcoming.

Parenting the Stretch Zone

Even though being a mom is one of the most critical aspects of my being, I also never felt more pressured, more judged, and more alone. The crazy thing was, most of those feelings came from my own thoughts about what parents were supposed to be. The boundaries I was willing to cross as an individual, I seemed less willing to allow my kids to cross. When I tried to be the overly protective parent, I realized it wasn't the authentic version of myself.

Recognizing that is the first step in understanding that, while your adventure stretches your own comfort zone, your kids will likewise be stretching your comfort zone for you. Allowing them to be in that stretch zone is critical to their development, too. Perfection is one of the negative stressors that we have to work against in getting outside the comfort zone. Kids need to experience challenges and work through adversity in order to build resiliency. It helps them think for themselves and creates opportunities for independence. It prepares them for the uncertainties they will experience in life and helps them strategize through risks that are all part of the world we live in. Don't we all want to raise confident, adaptable, resilient, independent kids? Adventure is one of the most versatile platforms to build those skills in a novel way.

Healing Properties of Adventure

One of my favorite lessons from 2020 was experiencing the healing properties of unstructured adventure play. Midweek, we'd walk away from everything and take a field trip to the woods with no agenda, no route, and no expectations. Week after week, the kids would find creative ways to play. They'd create forts, play out stories, and design tools to help them solve a problem. These were reassuring moments during vast uncertainty. The first time we did it, it was about the only forty-five minutes of that week that I had no responsibilities and could simply sit and breathe. The sounds of their play accompanied by the natural sounds of wildlife and nature was the most revitalizing experience to recalibrate my emotional state. When we came back to the house, I was able to plan dinner, support the next round of learning, and revisit my work.

Kids at young ages mirror the responses they see around them. When one of my kids gets hurt, I learned quickly that the more dramatic my response, the more dramatic their response. I still have the immediate *gasp and run response* built in, but it is also a trigger for me to take a deep breath and get into empathy mode ASAP. Managing my emotions in those moments of fear can be a great model for kids to understand how to manage their own fears and anxieties. It is definitely a lesson in noticing—being aware of how our thoughts and actions as a parent might be influencing our kids' thoughts and experiences.

We don't need to run in the rain or fall on a hike to have an adventure; both just happen to be stories of being discomfortable.

The critical phase is to recognize our mindset about new opportunities that challenge our ideas about safety. Being adventurous doesn't necessarily mean we do epic things outdoors. We just have to be willing to be a little less perfect, a little less comfortable, and a little more willing to take the next first step. With each step, we can assess the joy and decide if we want to step forward or leave the experience behind.

Key Takeaways

An adventure is a risky or uncomfortable experience. As you work through assessing risk, here are some questions to consider:

- What do I think adventure is? Remember the definition of *adventure* can be an undertaking involving danger or unforeseen risks *and* a new or remarkable experience.
- What limiting beliefs are you upholding? How can you flip a limiting belief such as "I'm not a reader" to "I read thirty books a year?"
- You do not need anyone's permission to do something that stretches you.
- What are your lessons in overcoming?
- Sharing experiences through the struggle leads to deeper connections. Whom have you shared a struggle experience with?
- Are you willing to participate in activities where you may not succeed?
- Risky play is critical to kids' development. How can you encourage getting your kid out of the upright position?
- Perfection disguised as safety and stability robs us of critical opportunities to raise confident, adaptable, resilient, and independent kids.

Sequence of Joy

"The joy we feel has little to do with the circumstances of our lives and everything to do with the focus of our lives."
—Russel M. Nelson

Through my journey in designing a life, I realized success was not a bunch of goals and boxes of achievements. It was a series of practices that require me to check in occasionally and make tweaks. Today, the "success" metric that I pay most attention to is joy. Far beyond any status symbol, title, or benchmark in life, my indicator of thriving became the sequence of joy.

Joy is often misunderstood and scientifically hard to measure. When I could embrace the joy each day and then stack joyful experiences, I began to experience the sequence of joy impact. Initially, I thought this was a little woo-woo; however, the more I practice this life and the more aware and in tune I am with my body, the more I have come to recognize the impact of joy in each segment of our life wheel. I don't believe it to be elusive or mystical in any way. In order for me to figure this out, I needed to redefine success and be aware of which elements of my life nurtured joy.

Slices of Pie

I imagine my day, week, month, or year as a pie; the pie represents my time and energy. Since time is a nonrenewable resource, I want to be aware of how I use mine. I also notice if the energy I expend during this time is associated with a negative experience, I spend much more time thinking about it. For example, if I had a disagreement or felt as though I wasn't treated with respect, I would often churn through the scenario or replay it in my mind. I might gather comments that I didn't make to use during the argument. I would spend significant time and energy thinking about the next negative experience I would have.

Triggers such as a comment on social media, a news heading we don't agree with, a friend's attack on our lifestyle can send us into a spiral of negative energy and time spent. Each of these eats away at our pies. They take a considerable amount of time and energy leaving very little available for the circumstances that provide the greatest joy in our lives. When I hear the term "life–work balance," I envision and question, *Why does work get 50% of the pie?*

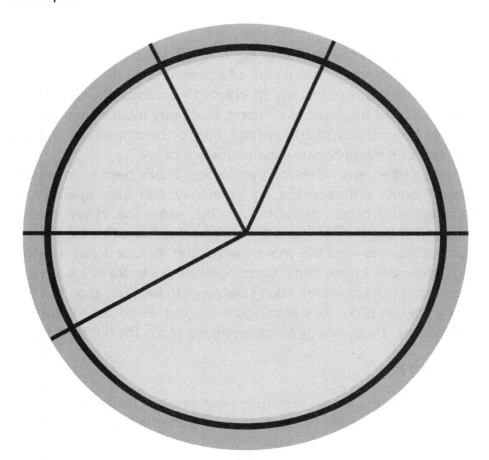

The Life Pie. Work is merely a slice of our life.
Who or What gets a slice of your life pie?

Joy is Abundant

The other key lesson is that while joy is not a limited resource, we can only accept as much joy into our lives as we are capable of receiving. As I tested the sequence of joy model, the feeling of guilt kept coming up. *Do I deserve to take this walk by myself? You have a really good job; you should be appreciative of what you have.* The inner critic was loud.

As Cait Flanders stated in her book *Adventures in Opting Out*, "We keep ourselves busy and do anything we can to avoid seeing the signs that are trying to point us in a different direction. Which means we are ignoring our truths." [6]

Joy is not a limited resource. When I experience joy, it doesn't mean there is less joy for others. We all deserve joy and happiness. The only factor that inhibits joy is our ability to receive it. Instead of chasing joy, which often looked like self-indulgent escapes with alcohol, shopping, or travel, I decided to instead focus on increasing my capacity to accept joy.

Increasing My Capacity to Accept Joy

I began by simply being aware.
- When did I experience joy today?
- If that was too challenging, I'd think more broadly: What was a joyful experience?
- What was joyful about the experience? Why?

The process reminded me of my time as a summer camp counselor and the creation of a happy list.

I spent several summers as a camp counselor at an overnight weeklong camp (I hear people call them sleep-away camps now). As camp counselors, we were often called upon to fill the dead space in the schedule with an activity, song, or game. These activities helped focus on the fun activities of camp and less on missing home. While sitting around one evening waiting for the next activity, we began sharing, "What are the things that make you happy?" Statements such as "Walking on a beach with really soft sand," "Getting seconds on your favorite ice cream," and "Having the sun warm up my face" began to fill the page. I noticed none of these were *things*. They were simple and accessible experiences, even for my broke lifestyle. I used the experience of creating the Happiness List as a basis for future intention-setting efforts.

I like to think of happiness as a temporary emotion or quick dopamine hit, often from an external source. Whereas joy is a sustained condition or state of being not based on circumstances or external influence. I am not here to police what is happiness and what is joy, only to make the distinction and recognize the difference. My big question became, how do I focus less on quick hits of happiness and focus more on living a life of joy?

As I strived through life, I learned it was not the *things* that brought joy. Things might have offered an initial dopamine spike to feel good, but it was generally not sustained. I began exploring other aspects of success relative to joy. Would status, power, and influence bring joy? The short answer was no, but it's hard to remember that in the land of productivity. The concept of joy is admirable, but is sustained joy realistic? How do I find joy?

The Joy Audit

You don't find joy; you create it. You embody it. One definition of joy is the emotion evoked by well-being, success, or good fortune. But how do you measure it?

I decided to embark on a family experiment to audit our family's joy. It was not meant to be an all-out research project, but I wanted to focus on joy as a critical element for our family to thrive. I used the following steps to help track both our individual and collective joy. While I don't anticipate you replicating this, I also know some people like to dig into the complexities of life. I am including a Joy Audit tool in the resource section to help you simplify this experiment on your own if you wish.

The Joy Audit was a framework I created that measured joy for our family. There were five elements I tracked each month, initially, but later determined each quarter was more reasonable. The five elements were:

1. What conditions led to highest-rated joy experiences?
2. What were the resources required? (Time and money were tracked.)

3. How did they rate their joy from the experience? Did it align with their expectations?
4. Would they recommend the experience to others (Net Promoter Score; Five-Star Review)?
5. Was the joy sustained after thirty days? After ninety days?

1. What are the conditions required for a joyful experience?

When designing any individual or family experience, I usually start with empathy. The intent with empathy is to get out of my thinking brain and into my feeling brain. This phase of the process helps cultivate the curiosity list. The intent is to generate options or experiences your family members have not done and to reveal ideas that excite them.

We include everything on the initial list. I don't think about time, money, or any layer of feasibility at this stage. I use this as a time to dream with all family members.

- What do they want to experience in life?
- What would they like to accomplish in life?
- What do they wish they had more time to do?
- What skills do they want to improve?
- What would an ideal day look like?

Make sure you do this process for yourself, too. I have done this with kids age three and older. If you have younger children, focus on the parents and older kids. Don't discredit options from the list for not being feasible in this phase. The critical part is to listen and encourage feelings versus rational thoughts.

During my empathy interview with our oldest, he revealed that he wanted to do an art project with me that he couldn't complete at home. He also preferred that his younger siblings weren't with him. He wanted to work on his project alone without interruptions. Perhaps a motherly projection, but I imagined having my full attention was also a condition of the experience he craved. As I explored what was possible, I remembered a unique experience I hadn't done since college—glass blowing. There is a glass museum about forty minutes from our house that offers workshops.

I found a glass-fusing workshop that he would be able to handle and signed us up.

Empathy as a Compass

Empathy and curiosity drive so many elements of our life now. Both empathy and curiosity are skills that can be improved with practice. My husband and I have date nights, dreaming about what we want our life to look like, and began to develop clarity around the steps to get there. Our kids each share ideas for projects or experiences that they'd like to try. Our seasonal adventure lists were a product of the empathy interviews.

Seasonal adventure lists compile mini-experiments and simple adventures we have an interest in testing the next three months. Each season, we document what we want to do to stretch ourselves into discomfortable. Ideas range from new adventures, destinations, or projects we want to try. Others are "minimum viable product" versions of a bigger, more elaborate desire. Several examples of our seasonal adventure lists are included in the resources section of this book.

For example, my husband revealed he has a dream to build or restore a car. We put it on the someday/maybe list. He realized it wasn't something he would likely do this year but something he wanted to work toward and learn more about. In his words, "I like that the kids are interested in learning about gears and motors, and I want to keep doing things to keep their interest going." His intention is to offer small ways to keep that interest alive.

One of the things I learned about my kids through this process is that they really appreciate one-on-one time with Mom and Dad. It makes them feel special. There are little details they share in these conversations that help me get to know them better and reveal undertones of their personality. It has also helped me better understand their love languages.

Love Languages

If you aren't familiar with the *The 5 Love Languages* by Gary Chapman,[7] I highly recommend diving in deeper. Designing experiences combining their interests while supporting them in their love language, allows us to share more meaningful experiences, thus, greater joy. These are the five love languages:

- <u>Quality Time:</u> Individuals with this love language value spending time together, particularly undivided attention from their loved ones.

- <u>Physical Touch:</u> Nonverbal communication often speaks louder than words. With this love language, body language and touch are comfortably used to express love.

- <u>Acts of Service:</u> These individuals believe actions speak louder than words and like to show others (and be shown by others) through acts of service that they are appreciated. (i.e., when someone goes out of their way to make your life easier by helping with chores or taking things off your plate.)

- <u>Words of Affirmation:</u> Actions don't always speak louder than words. This is a love language that values verbal acknowledgments of affection, compliments, appreciation, and encouragement.

- <u>Gifts:</u> Love is given and received through tangible items. It's not about the monetary amount but the symbolic thought behind the gifts.

Collectively, the discovery phase helps define what we could experience. I try to remind often that joy is not a destination or a thing. When I talk about adventure, most people jump to a "bucket list" filled with locations and destinations. If you get that as a response, dig deeper.

- What intrigues you about that location?
- Why do you want to go there?

Even the process of building the curiosity list is an intention to offer a shared experience. That intention and mindset of getting curious about the other person's thoughts and feelings, using empathy as a compass of discovery, was a key lesson for me in this process. And it's just the beginning.

2. What resources are required?

Time and money are tangible black and white metrics that we can attach to this experience.

- How long will it take to plan?
- How long will the actual experience last?
- How much did the experience cost?

In this step, we quantify the time and money needed for the ideal experience. We prioritize the feasibility or consider a version of the experience we might test in order to determine whether we keep the experience on this list.

There were many times when I would weigh an activity through the "Return on Investment (ROI) per experience" lens. I remember planning a family weekend to an indoor waterpark. We'd look for the best waterslides and spend a considerable amount of money staying in the adjoining lodge, yet most of the time, my kids simply played in the pool. We could easily go to a regular hotel with a pool, or if we wanted to focus on the activity that brought the most joy as well as a good return on investment, we could go to the local community pool for a fraction of the price. It's not always about being cheap but recognizing the crucial elements of the experiences that offer the greatest joy within our budget.

Often, when my husband and I would have date nights, we'd resist dinner and a movie because it didn't create an experience for deeper connection. A movie for two was easily a $25–$30 experience for us just to sit next to each other in a dark theater and stare at a screen. We realized we value an interactive experience.

One night, we decided the main element of our date would be to play laser tag. Yes, I'm sure the teenagers thought it was odd for a thirty-something-year-old couple to play countless rounds of laser tag, but it was a different experience that had us laughing and playing together. The ROI of joy from that unlimited round of laser tag for $30 was much greater than the joy from staring at a screen for two hours.

Hacking the Experience
We also like to take the big experiences from the dream list and test smaller pieces. My daughter has a strong desire and travel goal to visit all sixty-three (at the time of writing this) national parks. Knowing that would take years to accomplish, we decided to look at other ways to test aspects of the goal. Earlier this year, we

purchased an at-home escape room experience that took us on explorations through ten national parks. (The link is in the resources section.) The escape room took us several days to complete and revealed aspects of parks that we likely wouldn't have considered before completing the activity. It also reinforced a goal she is truly interested in accomplishing as well as put those parks at the top of our to-do list.

I have another child whose greatest joy would be to get a dirt bike. Any chance he gets to ask for a dirt bike, he goes for the jugular. It is quite honestly something my husband and I are not willing to budge on. For us, the cost is far greater than the potential reward, so we try to think about how we can offer a version of the experience without purchasing a dirt bike. (I should mention this child is currently five.)

We have friends who invite us to ride their dirt bikes. We have also attended dirt bike races, which still costs money, travel, and time, but it is still cheaper than buying a dirt bike. Another variation of the experience we have tested was creating mountain bike trails through the woods with jumps and turns to help simulate a dirt bike track. We have tried to demonstrate various ways to have a dirt-bike-like experience without having to purchase material things.

Much like auditing our spending, assessing our joy, or attaching the values to expenses, I have been able to set a benchmark for the ideal time/money ratio. It doesn't mean we don't do the expensive or quick ideas; we just might prioritize the options differently if we know what's on the list.

3. Rating joy

The rating scale can be whatever you choose. The most critical aspect of this is that the rating process is consistent. A consistent process allowed us to plot the data points and see what trends led to the greatest joy.

When we decided to embark on this Joy Audit, we tried to create the rating system as a family. There were no qualifiers for us on what defined a 1 versus what defined a 5. Because joy is an internal and individualized experience, we intended to get them into a feeling state to answer the questions most vividly. Yesterday, we did a bike ride down a major hill, through the park, and down a trail next to the river. Everyone gave the experience a 4 or 5 on the Joy Rating. When I asked why, these were some of their responses:

- I liked that the trail wasn't too hard.
- We got to play on the playground.
- It was the perfect day. Not too hot or cold, not too hard or too easy.
- I liked that we got ice cream. You let me get the sundae I wanted.
- Going down the big hill was really fun.
- It wasn't a long ride, but it could be longer.
- I liked that we did it all together.

Beyond the $18 for five ice cream items and the two hours spent on a new and different route through town, it was minimal time and money invested with a high-joy return. There was little whining or complaining, and I appreciated not only the great weather but the ability to get active and feel the strength of my body working. We all own bikes of varying types, so it was an experience that worked. And after a two-hour ride, it was easy to say yes to ice cream.

4. Reflections and Recommendations

In this phase, we explore what they learned and if they would recommend this experience to others. The first is a personal reflection: "What did you learn?" We try to design experiences that educate, inspire, and entertain. If none of the three was accomplished, we missed the boat. The flip side is that if we accomplished all three, that is a high-quality experience, a triple win!

During the reflection process, I also ask: "Was the Joy Rating what you expected?" In research, this is referred to as a post-pre assessment. The response to this question, especially with older kids, sparks conversation of about setting expectations and values. Reflection is a critical element of our adventures and important to completing the feedback loop.

A question businesses use to assess clients' satisfaction is: "Would you recommend the product or service to a friend or family member?" Standard tools used with many businesses are the Net

Promoter Score (NPS) and customer reviews. A Net Promoter Score is a survey format where customers rank several responses on a scale of one to ten. A Net Promoter Score of nine or ten would be considered loyal or repeat customers.

Businesses also use five-star reviews as the model for measuring whether clients would recommend their product or service. A review of four or five is a very positive customer experience. Both metrics are indicators of social proof. An organization, activity, or adventure with a high rating shows something about that experience left an immediate and favorable impression on the individual.

Our family uses the Joy Rating as a business would use Net Promoter Score or five-star review. A Joy Rating of four or five validates a joyful experience. The reflection and recommendation step establishes metrics that can be tracked over time.

5. Lasting impact

In terms of market scalability and impact, businesses usually look to see if the experience can be replicated and repeated. However, not everything needs to be replicated and repeated, and if it were, it doesn't always yield the same effect. Therefore, "Can the experience be repeated?" is only part of the question.

The bigger question is, "Did the experience have a lasting impact?" The way we measure lasting impact is to see which experiences they were still talking about thirty-plus days later. Interestingly, many memorable experiences had to do with things that didn't go according to plan or when something unexpected happened. Several could not be replicated, and if they were, they wouldn't have had the same level of impact.

Since the intention is to develop experiences that lead to joy, I want to come back to happiness vs. joy. An experience that had a high Joy Rating but was not discussed after thirty days (unprompted), was tagged as a happiness experience. A happiness experience is still helpful to our overall well-being. As discussed in an article from *Nurse Next Door*, "We need roughly five positive experiences to offset every one negative experience due to our tendency to lean unconsciously toward our negative bias."[8]

An experience that had high Joy Rating and was talked about (unprompted) beyond thirty-days was tagged as a joyful experience. A study by Lambert et al. (2012) found participants who shared their positive experiences (with a relationship partner) increased in positive affect, happiness, and life satisfaction over the course of four weeks."[9] Joyful experiences shared over time demonstrated deeper connection, meaning, or purpose.

Trial and Error

We tracked these five questions through planned-but-unexpected experiences. The Joy Audit gave us a framework to intentionally spend one-on-one time with each kid as well as collective family time. The goal was to have both a one-on-one and a full-family experience once a month (I'll explain how we planned these experiences in the Play Wildly section).

After each experience, both the parents and kids would individually journal or verbally answer the questions. The kids began sharing deeper things about their experiences that brought out both good and challenging feelings. They often ranked the one-on-one experiences highest and looked forward to them each month.

Interestingly, as a parent, I was trying to spend the same amount of money with each kid. However, I have one who likes to receive little things as part of the experience, while the other two prefer to focus on the spending time doing something they enjoy. Their love languages became more apparent, suggesting equal conditions did not create equal experiences. For this reason, we tried not to create too many rules around these experiences. We did encourage them to choose things that would be "worth it" in terms of experiences.

Through a series of trials, I realized authentic moments of joy were showing up more consistently in our lives while we were exploring the unknown and experiencing something new together. When life would get in the way and we skipped one-on-one time or spontaneous adventures, it was noticeable. The weight of everyday life would be more apparent in our sleeping, eating, and activity patterns.

On the flip side, the experiences with the longest-lasting impact were the simple things. Most of those experiences originated from one person's curiosity, which gave them a voice in selecting how joy might show up in our lives. We slowly saw the mindset shift from shopping or external things as part of the experience to topics of curiosity. We saw the shift from going somewhere to cultivating experiences at home. I am so grateful for this experiment for the simple fact that it slowed us down enough to notice and learn how to connect with our kids and create meaningful experiences in a time when life seemed to be racing by at breakneck speeds.

Inner Child

Experiencing joy is uniquely tied to awareness; many correlate it to contentment. I liken it to the feeling of being a happy-go-lucky little kid. Once, when I was in high school, my mom and I were coming home from a shopping excursion or some other mother–daughter day, and we were laughing about some silly thing. I remember us talking about the benefits of being a four-year-old. You are somewhat independent, you get to play, you love to learn, and you don't have all the responsibilities of life. And really, you are just naturally cute and cuddly, and people love to give you hugs and laugh at your jokes. (*Sigh, that sounds like a joyful life, doesn't it?*). We decided we wanted to be four on that day. We continue to look at each other periodically and say, "Let's be four today," and it's fun to transport ourselves back in time, let the pressures of life fizzle, and just enjoy the moment.

Earlier in the book, I mentioned to imagine life as a seven-year-old. The difference between four and seven is the amount of reason and responsibility you wish to exude. Some really struggle with age four being too playful. Age seven has been coined as "the age of reason." Developmentally at age seven, children develop the cognitive and emotional capabilities to control impulses and have rational thoughts. I suggest choosing the inner-child age that feels most appropriate for your circumstances.

In college, my friend Megan and I took a spontaneous road trip from Wisconsin to Memphis and then over to Oklahoma. Through a series of random and unplanned events, we ended up with a bobblehead iguana on the dash of the new-to-me Dodge Stratus we were driving. Our bobblehead had several names, but for the sake of this story, we will call him Iggy. We would occasionally ask Iggy yes or no questions and let the motion of Iggy's head be the answer to inform where we would go. On one of our stops, we asked Iggy if we should go to Graceland. His head bobbed up and down, and we obliged. The route from Wisconsin to Oklahoma, by way of Memphis, was not rational. Letting a bobblehead iguana determine our route, was not rational. Embracing our inner child, we created shared experiences we still talk about.

As a mom, it's easy to lose myself in the responsibilities of daily life. When I look at the experiences that created lasting joy in my own life, there is a theme of playfulness. When I can drown the outside noise and just be in the moment. Joy is most present in my life when I am most present—when I can focus where my feet are.

Since joy is an internal state, experiencing it is very personal and unique to the individual. What matters to me is having the basis for individual and collective joy. The freedom to be authentically joyful in your skin is the most liberating and gratifying experience. Yet it's not an experience I have regularly. Sharing experiences with someone who has the same caliber for joy is icing on the cake—it is helpful to pay attention who is around you when you experience both individual and collective joy. It's worth noting our tribes as we design our life practice.

Dependency

As a mom, I found myself in an interesting place as a giver. There are many times I was so focused on cultivating joy in others that it was sometimes at the detriment of my own joy. I was slipping into periods of temporary happiness as opposed to a deeper state of joy. I began putting false expectations on joy and framing it as a summit instead of a journey. I was so focused on creating joyful experiences for others that I began to lose the best version of myself. Even though I was doing all the things right on the outside (some might say I was crushing it), I was codependent on my husband and kids, finding joy for them before I allowed myself to experience it.

In due time, I was able to turn this around. One day I was sitting in an airport in Texas. My younger son was under two years old, and for whatever reason, he was in a state of despair. His bottom lip was thick, his eyes clenched tightly, and a very loud bellow of disapproval burst from his little mouth. I knew everything about the moment was outside my control, and I embraced it with a relatively calm demeanor. My initial flustered frustration fizzled to contentment.

I couldn't help but chuckle slightly, wanting to remember that moment. My son was so in alignment with his feelings, and there was no guesswork needed. There was nothing I could do to fix it. He needed to feel it and go through the motions before I could offer any manner of support.

As I observed and allowed his moment of two-year-old despair to pass, a stranger walked up and said, "You are an amazing mom. I have seen many moms and children in my years, and most moms rush to hush and fix. You are allowing him to feel."

I was stunned. I didn't plan that moment. I couldn't create the conditions. All I could do was be aware of my own thoughts and feelings and allow my son to feel his. The power of that moment was not that I didn't react to my son's meltdown; it was that my joy wasn't determined by his.

The Joy of Imperfection

Joy is an inner feeling and may not look perfect on the outside. I realized that as a mom, I needed to have a state of individual joy that was not determined by the collective or individual joy of others. If you are a people pleaser, this is an important step in noticing your thoughts and feelings. We cannot expect our family to be the source of our joy. They can trigger moments of happiness, but joy is fostered from within and is a prolonged sense of being. I sometimes need to remind myself: *I can be the best version of myself even when things are out of my control; my joy is not dependent on someone else's joy and likewise someone else's joy is not dependent on mine.*

Our ability to accept joy and love in our life requires us to be open to receiving it. I know many who can contribute joy and love, but they struggle to receive it from others. You deserve joy. When we increase our capacity to accept joy, we also calm our mind.

As Brené Brown found, "Joy is the most vulnerable emotion we experience. And if you cannot tolerate joy, you start dress rehearsing tragedy." Dress rehearsing tragedy, she explains, is imagining something bad is going to happen when in reality, nothing is wrong. Brown found in her research that people who have a capacity for joy are particularly good at taking it in. She says that "instead of using [joy] as a warning to start practicing disaster, they used it as a reminder to practice gratitude."[10]

Capacity for Receiving Joy

Understanding joy as an internal state is a healthy reminder that I cannot bring my kids joy by trying to fix or buying things for them. The best thing I can do is help them feel their feelings and recognize the size of their joy mail slot. When we understand the power of our thoughts, we give permission to the power of our feelings. Our thoughts control our feelings.

I am still learning this and recognize that when I am in a bad place and my thoughts are taking me down the drain, I often experience feelings of anger and despair. To counter this pattern, first I notice it, then I begin to work through a process of changing my thoughts. Here are some of my early checkpoints:

- What am I feeling?
- What am I thinking that is causing me to feel this way?
- Why do I think that is true?
- What triggered this thought?
- What is another thought that could be true?

Questioning our thoughts is common in coaching practices. My friend uses the expression "Name it to tame it." The bulk of our thoughts happen subconsciously. When we ask ourselves questions (such as these) we disrupt the sequence subconsciously holding thoughts, beliefs, values, and behaviors in place.

One of the reasons I like adventure is that it gives us a distraction, a means and a purpose for play to challenge our minds and bodies in different ways. I can't always think and talk out what I am feeling, but I find great clarity from fresh air and freedom. For me, adventure opens the mail slot to accept joy and share gratitude more freely. Every once in a while, it's helpful to write down a few thoughts about joy in your own life. Some refer to them as gratitude prompts. They are great tools to help recalibrate yourself and get out of the quicksand—and to set the stage for where you want your feet to be today.

I have noticed that when I am not in a state of joy and contentment, it is because I am allowing the other critics to consume my thoughts. It's easy to think about all the possible scenarios and begin to play out the bad ones in our heads. As referenced earlier, Brené Brown referred to this as "dress rehearsing tragedy." We will dive deeper into the feeling of fear and how to disrupt subconscious thoughts holding fear in place in the next chapter.

Key Takeaways

Joy is a journey not a destination. Through a series of experiences, you get better at learning when you feel most joyful. As you work through the sequence of joy, here are some questions to consider:

- When did I experience joy today?
- What was joyful about the experience? Why?
- In the Joy Audit framework, the following questions establish metrics for measuring joy:
- What conditions led to the highest-rated joy experiences?
- What were the resources utilized when testing experiences?
- How did they rate their joy from the experience?
- Did the experience align with their expectations?
- Would they recommend the experience to others?
- Was the joy sustained after thirty days?
- To counter feelings inhibiting joy, I use the following questions:
- What am I feeling?
- What am I thinking that is causing me to feel this way?
- Why do I think that is true?
- What triggered this thought?
- What is another thought that could be true?

Working through Fear

"May your choices reflect your hopes, not your fears."
—Nelson Mandela

One of the most vulnerable feelings we can have is joy because it's immediately followed by fear and shame. We jump from a joyful state to the worst-case scenarios. We can't live in our thoughts or we might never take action. However, fear isn't something we can just get over; we need to face our fears and work through them. Ironically, several worst-case scenarios have happened to me, and they were never as bad as I thought they would be.

As a mom of young kids, I never wanted to be *that family* with the crying, obnoxious kids on an airplane. We traveled with all our kids as infants through the toddler stage and beyond. I often felt the stares of what I perceived to be resentment from what I imagined other passengers thought about us.

One early morning, as we left the hotel for a 6 a.m. flight, I had this sense that things were off. No one slept particularly well the night before, which is never a great start to a traveling day with young children. As I approached the ticket counter to check in, my three-year-old indicated she felt sick, just as the ticket agent requested my six-month-old's birth certificate for the lap seat ticket.

Panic. I didn't have it.

"Mom, I think I need to throw up!"

Panic. A mad dash for the doors to get outside.

I returned to the ticket counter as my husband was scrambling to find any medical record online with our youngest's date of birth.

"What is the worst-case scenario if we can't find a medical record with his birthdate?" I asked the woman working the ticket counter.

"I would need to charge you full-fare for the ticket," she replied.

"And what is the full-fare cost?"

An astronomical amount came out of her mouth. My stomach sank, and I was so mad at myself for not even thinking about packing the birth certificate.

"Mommy!" Half crying, half screaming, my daughter called for help just before she threw up all over the floor.

I felt completely defeated.

"It's taken care of, Miss," the ticket agent politely offered from across the ticket counter.

My throat felt tight, and my eyes got blurry. "Thank you," I said gratefully while attempting to clean the vomit from the floor. The airport staff assured me that a cleaning crew was coming, and I did not need to stay and clean the floor.

As we made our way through security, another round of sickness hit, and once again, I was mortified and quickly began trying to clean it up.

That time, an airport staff member stopped me and said, "Miss, this is our job. Your job is to go comfort your daughter." She handed me some garbage bags and paper towels just in case and sent us on our way.

Stunned, I followed her orders. As we boarded the plane, I was dripping with bags and blankets from both arms, my daughter unfortunately came running up the aisle. "Mom, I need to..."

I desperately grasped at the bag, and two passengers on either side of the aisle pulled it open for me. Another passenger gathered my daughter's long hair and put it in a scrunchie from her wrist. I was watching the kindness and generosity of strangers swarm us over and over again. These were the same people I thought resented us.

My thoughts were not true.

That overly adventurous and less-than-desirable start to our trip proved to be one of the greatest moments of overwhelming support from complete strangers.

Worst-Case Scenario

How often do we believe false narratives, thus denying ourselves the opportunity to let go and just experience the moment? We give fear and doubt the power to make decisions on our behalf. In reality, even if the worst-case scenario happens, it's still a valuable experience.

I lived through a worst-case scenario while downhill skiing in Upper Michigan. We had been skiing for years, and the kids were quite proficient, regularly skiing blue (intermediate) and black diamond (expert) ski runs in Wisconsin. As my daughter and I boarded the ski lift for one more run, her ski got caught on my ski. It pulled her down as the lift swung through, so she couldn't board the ski lift. I grabbed her to pull her up, but her butt was below the seat, and I couldn't lift her any further, nor was she able to reach back to pull herself up. The ski lift operator didn't see this struggle, as we rose higher and higher. I was yelling "Stop!" over and over, yet the lift continued to ascend while my daughter dangled. We were nearly twenty feet high before the lift stopped. That was the worst-case scenario I had played out in my head so many times when we were teaching our kids how to ski.

My daughter calmly said, "Mom, I'm scared."

In my head, I was scared too, but I confidently replied, "I am going to hold on. I love you and will hold on as long and as tight as I can. It will be really hard for me to hold you if you get scared and start thrashing around, so I need you to trust me and stay as calm as possible."

We had practiced mindfulness, so we both took a deep breath to relax our bodies enough to keep the physiological response of fear at bay. The next part is interesting. An army of people ran toward us. I could hear the commotion below, and I knew my husband was among the crew working on our rescue. They asked my daughter to drop her poles. Then they hoisted one of the staff up the ladder of the chairlift tower of the chairlift where we had conveniently stopped. He was able to remove her skis.

Eventually, when it was time, they asked me to let go. Even writing this, I can feel all the feelings. Requesting a mother to let go of her daughter as she dangled over twenty feet in the air and trust that it would be okay is a lot to ask. I did it. I let go and dropped her into a basket of people who caught her and gently cradled her into the deep snow below. There was a moment of silence, and then my daughter revealed a bit of a smirk and chuckle, "That was kinda fun!" The army of helpers all took a deep breath and sighed.

We both ran back to our comfort zones and took the time to recharge before we were willing to take another ski run. While we were all in the panic zone during that experience, it taught us so many things about ourselves and each other and about how to manage discomfort and fear. Yet it still took both my daughter and me a bit to get back on the ski lift. We did it slowly and with much more awareness.

Preparing for Fear

Interestingly, my husband watched a YouTube video about a ski lift rescue a week before our incident, so he was ready with several rescue options. When we think ahead to possible uncomfortable scenarios, we take extra steps to be mentally prepared for them. Since then, we have also learned to be advocates for ourselves.

That particular ski lift was pretty fast and hit the back of our legs lower than normal. We could have asked the lift operator to slow it down, but we didn't want to bother him or be a pain to expect other skiers to accommodate our discomfort. However, now we pay attention to when we are uncomfortable, and we aren't afraid to ask for these things.

Our kids continue to practice telling us when they are nervous or afraid, so we can adapt or scale back the adventure to a threshold that stretches them without getting too close to the panic zone. I didn't want the fear of that experience to rob my daughter and me of future years skiing. Together, we shared an experience in overcoming the worst-case scenario.

It's not always up to us to solve our fears. We acknowledge when fear is the main feeling. We explore how to scale back. Then we step into gratitude. We appreciate fear as part of our story because it has given us a memorable connection. My daughter and I can now talk about how grateful we are for what we worked through and how many people were there to support us.

I tell you these stories to share that even when the worst-case scenario happens, the outcome probably won't turn out as bad as the scenario you create in your head. My worst-case experiences brought out the greatest traits of humanity: kindness, generosity, and compassion. My fears were merely a figment of my imagination. I am not advocating that we be dismissive of our fears; rather, it is wiser that we be in tune with our fears.

Fear-Setting

Our family is intrigued about long-term family travel. We are excited about the freedom and flexibility; however, we don't want to jeopardize our safety or stability. We needed a way to assess our adventure risk tolerance, to think through potential uncomfortable scenarios and feel confident with our decisions. A tool to determine which fears were valid and which fears we could neutralize.

Tim Ferris is an American entrepreneur and author best known for his book, *The 4-Hour Work Week*. He attributes much of his success to stoicism after struggle for years with trauma and mental illness and suicide attempts. The lessons of Seneca, an ancient Stoic philosopher, suggest our adversities are actually benefits. Tim used these teachings to develop the fear-setting framework.

The fear-setting framework, highlighted by Tim Ferris in his Ted Talk,[11] helped name our fears and work through thoughts and feelings to validate or neutralize fear. These are the steps to this framework:

A. **What if I...** Identify the decision you are trying to make.
B. **Define.** Make a list of ten to twenty fears you have related to that decision.
C. **Prevent.** Write what you could do to avoid that fear coming true. Do this for each fear listed in the Define section.
D. **Repair.** If the fear came true, what would you do? Make a list of all the things you could do to make the fear scenario better.

As an example, the Fear-Setting graphic on the next page walks through the fears we have about long-term family travel.

What decision are you stuck on?

Our family of five would like to travel for several months

DEFINE	PREVENT	REPAIR
list 10-20 fears keeping you stuck	how could you prevent the fear from coming true?	If it came true, what would you do?
Run out of money We miss our friends and family We fight more We get sick or hurt while traveling Taking care of the house while away Kids fall behind (learning/activities) What if something happens to a loved one back home	Run out of money • track spending and keep expenses as close to life expenses as possible (Not a vacation mindset) • Have major expenses booked and paid for before we leave • Have emergency fund and opportunity fund with 3-6 months expenses. • Have active income while traveling	Run out of money • Use mid-term savings (brokerage) fund to cover expenses • Use Roth contributions to cover expenses • Come home • Create an opportunity to sell (Side hustle) • Get a Job (Cash, seasonal, remote • borrow money (credit cards)

The Science of Fear

Fear is a physiological response to a negative stressor. The negative stressor in fear is more often triggered by a thought as opposed to an external source. From the scientific perspective, an external source perceived to be dangerous triggers the brain to release chemicals to the nervous system. The chemicals are often "stress hormones," such as adrenaline, kicking us into high gear, making the body tense and alert. At the same time, the nervous system is turning down nonessential systems (like our immune and digestive systems) to put all the energy toward addressing the emergency. Do you ever notice your stomach churn when you get nervous? Other physiological things are also happening, such as increased heart rate and blood pressure, pupils dilating to allow more light in, and veins constricting to keep blood in the major muscle groups.

The sequence is commonly known as fight-or-flight response and was designed to put the body on high alert with the ability to respond quickly. Throughout history, the physical dangers we face have declined, but our bodies still respond in fight-or-flight mode for modern-day fears. It is important to know that the brain essentially loses the ability to make rational thoughts while in a state of fear.[12]

In addition to the adrenaline being released, the brain releases dopamine, which is known as the feel-good hormone. We might know someone who thrives on activities that cause fear in others. Often known as thrill seekers, they might crave the highest roller coasters or choose adventures that push the boundaries of safety. These individuals seek fight-or-flight responses in order to experience the cocktail of adrenaline and dopamine.

The key to keeping our fears in check is to notice our thoughts and feelings. Since we don't make rational thoughts when in the fight-or-flight mode, we might need to get back into the comfort zone to allow our brain time to process, or lean on others who are not in the fight-or-flight mode to make rational decisions. Learning the boundaries of discomfort and panic is critical, as is adjusting to allow people to mentally retreat when they experience fear. Pushing their boundaries in the panic zone does more harm than good.

Mindfulness

After a prolonged state in the stretch zone, or any time in the panic zone, our body is overstimulated. We need to come back to the comfort zone to reset and rejuvenate. I recognized I wasn't always following the principles of joy. Instead, I would look for a quick dopamine hit from an external source to feel better. The external sources for me were a drink with friends, shopping for something new, or a physical escape to a new or different place. This was an escape not a reset. I returned to the same anxious overwhelm that triggered my fear. I skipped the step to determine whether my fear was unfounded.

If you describe a rumor, belief, or feeling as unfounded, it means that it is wrong and not based on facts or evidence. The fear-setting process helped me work through the steps to determine whether my fears had merit, but I needed to get my brain out of fight-or-flight mode and into a comfortable state. The solution for me was mindfulness.

Mindfulness is a practice to deescalate the stress response, and return to our comfort zone. It disrupts subconscious thoughts holding fear in place. Mayo Clinic defines mindfulness as a meditation practice "in which you focus being intensely aware of what you're sensing and feeling in the moment, without interpretation or judgment. Practicing mindfulness involves breathing methods, guided imagery, and other practices to relax the body and mind to help reduce stress."[13]

Mindfulness guides us through how to breathe, to calm our mind and body. The most accessible tool we have is our breath. I use a free app (Healthy Minds) to guide me through practices. Each night, I listen to guided meditations with my kids using the app. It helps us deescalate from everyday life and prepare for a state of rest. As referenced in the ski lift story, my daughter was familiar with mindfulness, and we were able to use the practice while dangling twenty feet in the air. Using mindfulness following fear helps us return to our comfort zone.

From a mindset perspective, focusing on what is possible will help guide the next step and different options to achieve success.

A way back to comfort and joy is to practice mindfulness and gratitude. Some fears are unfounded. Testing the boundaries of discomfort and listening to your body's physiological response will help determine when to forge ahead and when to retreat.

Key Takeaways

The human brain is not designed for rational thoughts in fight-or-flight mode. When we are stuck in fear, here are things to remember:

- Fear is not a "bad" feeling; it's designed to protect us from the panic zone. Are you in danger? If not, explore the following steps to disrupt your thoughts and calm your body.
- What if I... Identify the decision you are trying to make.
- Define. "Name it to tame it," as my friend would say. Make a list of ten to twenty fears related to the decision. Include any fear, big or small, contributing toward being stuck.
- Prevent. What can I do to prevent this fear from coming true? Brainstorm all of the ways you could prevent the list of fears from coming true.
- Repair. If the fear came true, what would you do? Make a list of all the things you could do to make the outcome better.
- Do you seek external sources and escape? How do you reset after fear?
- The ROI on mindfulness is exponential. How else can you claim profound impact for free?

Part 2: Explore Bravely

Perceptions of Success

"Little hinges swing big doors."
—W. Clement Stone

Society and consumerism like to try to sell us on the idea that success is achieved once you reach a certain status, own certain things, or achieve a certain goal. However, many of these definitions of success only reflect one dimension of our life (such as career, work, or money). It is difficult to claim success in all dimensions at one time, but it is easy to stay stuck in those that are most comfortable for us to achieve success.

Metrics of Thriving

A tool that was helpful for me in getting a sense of what success looks like in all dimensions of life is the Wheel of Life tool. I'll give an overview of the tool in this section; however, I adapted the tool, which is available in the resources section. The tool divides your life into six different dimensions. I like to select categories that mean the most to me that I feel I need for a whole and centered life, so I start with a blank wheel. The list of categories might include the following:

- Career and Work
- Money
- Health and Well-Being
- Recreation and Play
- Hobbies and Creativity
- Social Life, Friends, and Relationships
- Family
- Partnership and Intimacy
- Personal Growth and Development
- Spirituality

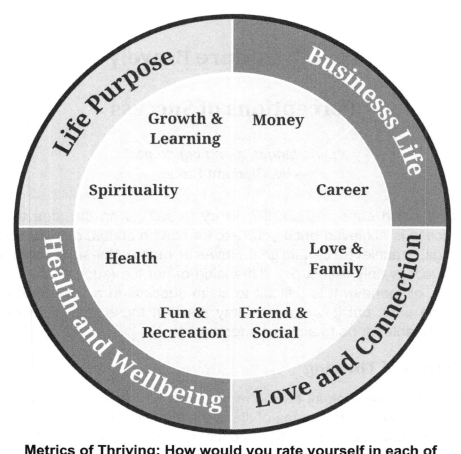

Metrics of Thriving: How would you rate yourself in each of these slices?
Where do you want your rating to be in the future?

Feel free to make more slices or use different words for the categories. I suggest you define each section in a way that works best for you rather than finding the perfect tool. Don't get hung up on the words. Focus on the dimensions of life that are important for you to have in order to thrive.

The purpose of this tool is to do a self-assessment and create a practice. Begin by rating yourself in each dimension on a scale of 1–10. One means you are the least satisfied with your life; ten means you have achieved a level of satisfaction that aligns with your definition of thriving. Don't overthink it; just go with your first response. To turn these ratings into a visual representation, plot each rating. A rating of one is on the center of the circle, a five rating halfway to the edge of the circle, and a ten is on the outer edge of the circle. Plot each rating accordingly, then connect the dots around the circle.

For a long time, I thought "balance" meant I was a ten in all dimensions of life. It turns out that is unrealistic and unsustainable. We need times of struggle to reclaim our joy. There are also seasons of life when a four is just going to have to do, and that is okay. The ratings are personal and not intended to be compared to others. As many say, "Comparison is the thief of joy."

I spoke with an entrepreneur who was doing really well in career and work but desired growth in other dimensions of his wheel. However, he didn't have a clear understanding of what would get him from a five to an eight in the family dimension. He found himself shifting back into career and work on a regular basis, even though he already hit all the metrics to be at eight or nine. Our natural tendencies are to fall back into what is most comfortable to us or the aspects of our life where we have developed a skill set.

Hacking Frameworks of Success

Rather than starting from scratch, I encourage you to use the frameworks in which you are already successful and apply them to other areas of your life.

- If your superpower is finance, apply accounting principles to your time and energy. What would a Profit and Loss statement look like with energy as your currency? I once took an investment portfolio and applied it to our relationships and friends. Which asset classes did we want to have the greatest exposure to, and how much of my time should be invested in those relationships?
- If you are familiar with an International Standards Organization (ISO) environment, which is used to establish critical standards to improve business credibility, how do you

apply the process and procedures to optimize your health and well-being practices?

- If you are very strong in the spiritual sector, apply the learnings and scriptures to family life.

I have a friend who used the skills he had practiced in project management and applied them to writing a book (incidentally, the book is titled *Project Management for Writers* by Terry Stafford. If you have the urge to write a book, it's a great framework).

Be cautious to not become complacent or overfocused on one segment without recognizing the implications in other segments. I know several people who overfocus on their career in their thirties only to realize they neglected their health in the process.

Authentic Adventures

Western culture will regularly encourage you to want more. *They* will want you to work more. *They* want you to buy more. *They* want you to associate high value with high dollars. What is fascinating is the basis for this is most often grounded in fear of safety and stability. As I dug deeper, I learned that no one really knows or can identify who *they* are. It is an elusive group of voices the person thought to be true.

The other thing I find interesting is that in working with high-wealth individuals, none of them felt safer when they made more money. More often, I heard they had more to lose or spent more money keeping their assets safe. Be aware of which voices you are listening to.

What do you actually value, and is that where you are spending your time and money? After my second child was born, I realized I was choosing a path that was different from other moms and professionals I knew. At the same time, I felt like I was leaning into my true self. I wanted those around me to feel like they could be uniquely themselves around me. I think that is the definition of authenticity.

Untourism

My husband had only flown once before meeting me. While he was open to the idea of travel, it wasn't something he saw value in. We agreed to a travel budget of $2,500 for the year for a family of four (at the time). I wanted him to experience some of the magic I had experienced from travel without being stressed about money. Other families in our network believed travel was expensive or something you waited to do when the kids were older. I wanted to prove that traveling with young kids was not only possible but also affordable.

I designed authentic travel experiences based on the interests of our family without the overpriced bells and whistles. I now call this type of travel "untourism." These were simple adventures meeting new people, discovering local flavors, and exploring natural wonders for a fraction of most families' travel budgets.

I remember sitting in nosebleed seats at a Seattle Mariners stadium when my husband looked at me and said, "I get it now. I understand why we need to travel as a family." We spent the day exploring unique sites of the city. We arrived at the game early to watch batting practice when our son was called down to the front row to be given a ball from a player. The kids were laughing and dancing throughout the game. We devoured garlic fries as our third-inning snack. We weren't checking items off a bucket list. We were designing authentic travel experiences to allow us to connect as a family, spending money only on the things we valued.

Setting Expectations

Many parents my age grew up in a time when expectations for educational benchmarks or sports achievements were high. Expectations can be a negative stressor when the pressure stifles the ability to take the next step. If the high expectations and benchmarks feel unattainable, the individual can be thrust into a distress mode. It can become debilitating and have negative consequences on health and well-being. However, high expectations can also be motivators that encourage individuals to push themselves to a higher level of achievement.

I feel lucky that in my youth I rarely felt pressured to reach high expectations. Instead, it was my own curiosity that led me to go after high expectations. However, that internal desire somehow shifted over the past twenty years to where achievement became ingrained in my identity. I almost feared who I would become if I didn't achieve. For twenty-plus years, I put the success metrics of Career and Money on a higher pedestal than the other areas of my life and allowed someone else to decide what my next goal was. I became addicted to achieving. With each new expectation, I lost a little more curiosity. I had to recalibrate my definition of success and align my expectations, using joy as my compass for all the spokes in my Wheel of Life.

Windows of Opportunity

There are aspects to our lives that have an expiration date. No matter how hard we try, my three-year-old will turn four, and with each new year comes a new stage of growth and experiences to share. I can't conveniently turn back when I'm fifty and try to relive life the way I wish I could when my kids were age six, four, and one. I also didn't feel the need to wait for the kids to be at a certain age to pursue the adventures we wanted to experience as a family. All of the joyful experiences we began testing as a family confirmed we were on the path that was right for us.

When my husband and I were first dating, we had a long-distance relationship and spent several minutes on the phone every few nights.

One night while chatting, I said, "I can't wait until the end of the month. I hope these next few weeks go fast." We had planned to see each other then, and at the start of summer, he planned to move closer to me.

In response, he wisely stated, "Heidi, you have to stop wishing your life away. The day will come when we will be together."

I can't tell you how many times in the middle of the night, while up with an unhappy baby, I caught myself wishing for the stage to be over, only to stop and take a deep breath. "Enjoy this moment.

Stop wishing your life away," I'd tell myself. A few years later, when a child's challenging attitude found its way into a family conversation, I stopped and reminded myself that someday I'd want their authentically honest opinion. Don't wish this life away.

Those were lessons that taught me that joy doesn't only come from the good things that happen in our lives. It goes back to the definition of happiness in comparison to joy. So often, those "good things" are external triggers to a short-term feeling. Joy is a state of contentment influenced by our own internal elements. Catching myself grateful for the lack of sleep, for not seeing my boyfriend for weeks, or the flare of an attitude were moments when I realized that joy was not conditional. The periods of struggle helped accentuate the joy.

Saying No

As someone who craves connection and loves to experience new things, saying no became a new adventure. Ironically, a strange thing occurred. When I believed in my *no*, my *yes* became so much more powerful. The Joy Audit experiment gave me clarity about when I needed to say no. If I couldn't say, "Hell yes," then I needed to believe in my *no*.

A fascinating discovery was also revealed. When I stopped the laser focus on my career and money and began working on success metrics in the other spokes of my life, my career and money situation improved, too. If you rely on someone else's definition of success, you might look back with regret and wonder if it was all worth it.

The bigger question is, what does success look like for you and your family? Are those expectations motivating or creating pressure to be something that isn't aligned with your joy? When you align your definition of success and elevate the joy experiences for you and the members of your family, you are in better alignment with the multi-dimensional nature of your life.

Key Takeaways

Thriving is a multi-dimensional formula that relies on nourishment in the many spokes in your Wheel of Life. Here are some checkpoints to determine your metrics of thriving:

- What dimensions of your life do you prioritize?
- What dimensions of your life currently rate below a five? Are you okay with that?
- How can you utilize expertise you have success with, and apply the lens to other dimensions of life?
- What opportunities are a "Hell yes?"
- What does success look like for you and your family?
- Are the expectations of success motivating or creating pressure to be something that isn't aligned with your joy?

Needing Money

*"Americanism: We buy things we don't need
with money we don't have to impress people
we don't like."*
—Robert Quillen

"But joy doesn't pay the bills!" I hear you, and I feel you.

There were days I was so stinking high on life only to come down to reality and the bills that lay on the counter staring at me. I developed an unhealthy strategy. When life felt heavy, I would do whatever I could to escape, which for me was an adventure or traveling. That might seem innocent, but it also became a crutch to avoid dealing with the issues in front of me. Rather than using the time away to create clarity, I used it to ignore reality, so coming down was always hard. In many ways, it still is hard.

Remember that best-worst year I had? When I decided to leave my job and put my house up for sale? I didn't have another job, and I owed so much money on the house. I had to cash in a small mutual fund, plus take out a personal loan using a lien against my car, in order to bring enough money to the closing—aaand I accepted an offer that was $13,000 more than what I paid for it. It's hard to believe there was a silver lining to that.

The silver lining came in the form of hindsight. In the process of figuring out the details of my departure from that stage of life, I had overlooked an old checking account I hadn't closed. When a check I hadn't posted hit the account, it resulted in a negative balance. I saw the overdraft notices, but I was so worried about keeping things afloat that I just ignored them, hoping they would magically go away. After almost three months, I finally had to face it and ended up paying over $600 in fees for an original $25 overdraft charge.

Magnifying the Problem

When we procrastinate and worry, we magnify the problem, which usually ends up costing us more. If I had faced that issue head-on and tackled it on day one, I could have prevented the compounding effect of the worry. While there was a financial impact, I sometimes think we allow the financial currency the power to override our energy currency. The energy currency I spent on a $600 problem was definitely more costly mental energy I dedicated to solving (or rather, avoiding) that problem.

The irony in all of this was that in 2008, I was hired to design youth development programs, and the greatest need was youth financial literacy programming. Fortunately, I was hired for my ability to design programs for youth, *not* for my financial practices! They had confidence in me that I didn't have in myself.

Teaching and Learning

Teaching about money forced me to learn things outside my comfort zone, plus my money story made me more relevant to young adult audiences. I began to review studies on behavioral economics, spending patterns, financial benchmarks, critical life decisions, and the costs associated with them. I was living through what many young people never learn.

Although I could stretch a dollar in creative ways, the thought of actually understanding the numbers felt daunting. I could no longer keep kicking the YOLO (You Only Live Once) can down the road, hoping all my financial challenges would go away. I began turning to gurus in personal finance.

My comfort zone grew.

I paid closer attention to where I was spending money. I decided to practice tracking life costs and implementing strategies like the debt snowball, challenging myself to get uncomfortable (and then comfortable) with strategies such as having five to seven streams of income, as a means to take control of my financial life.

The beautiful thing about money is that it's math, and there is always an answer. What does your life actually cost? Today, it's easier than ever to figure it out by using financial technology tools, many of which are embedded directly into our accounts. Knowing my numbers was a large deposit in my energy bank account.

They say knowledge is power. I would say that is only true if you do something with it. I wasn't going to be a meticulous budget person. I had a sense of how much our life costs and could make informed decisions comparing our spending with our Joy Audit. Could we spend less in certain areas? Could we create revenue in other areas? How could we optimize our life? Knowing our numbers and seeing opportunities for growth gave me the energy and desire to chase the margins.

Our Money Story

In each segment of our budget, we made value decisions. I can stretch a dollar in clothing, groceries, and experiences, as well as repurpose rummage sale items a hundred different ways. Whereas my husband is the DIY-guy extraordinaire who can build, fix, and maintain things around the home. So initially, most of the money equation came on the "decrease spending" side because those were our strengths. But growth happens in the zone of discomfort.

Our money story changed when we got serious about our income. We got better at negotiating and not settling for the status quo. We doubled down on our debt, and in due time maxed out contribution limits into all our retirement accounts. We automated our savings and bills, so we wouldn't attach emotions to our finances, and we made sound decisions upfront based on our values and energy currencies for both income and expenses.

Rules for Our Money Relationship

Although my husband and I are both listed on each other's accounts, we maintained separate checking accounts and managed our own money. Since we came into the relationship with our own methods for managing our money, we created two simple rules for our monetary relationship around money that helped us remain transparent and make big decisions together.

1. We discuss with each other any purchase over $250. That was a spending threshold we felt was fair to discuss with

others. It was usually on one item. We didn't micromanage the rules of the other person's spending.
2. When one of us shares an idea, the other cannot say no to it for twenty-four hours. This requires both parties to really determine if the idea was truly something we valued or it was FOMO creeping in. This includes everything from a big purchase, a home renovation project, or a vacation.

Both rules give us more time and space between the stimulus and the response. Creating this space when making spending decisions has proven helpful.

Financial Independence

I was introduced to financial independence through the *Choose FI* podcast hosted by Jonathan Mendonsa and Brad Barrett. I binge listened to their thoughtfully curated content, then took action steps to improve my money story, which built my confidence with money. I was so enamored by the concept of simplicity that it completely changed the next phase of my life.

Financial independence is a money framework based on several key principles:

- Income minus expenses is the gap to invest. The goal is to grow the gap and invest in opportunities for compound interest. To grow the gap, we can increase income and/or reduce or/sustain spending. If we increase our income and increase our spending, the gap to invest is not growing.
- The formula for financial independence is 25x your yearly expenses. The first step was defining our actual life costs, then multiplying by twenty-five.
- The total is the amount needed to save to reach financial independence (FI) and not be required to generate new income each year. The formula is based on a 4% safe withdrawal rate. The total multiplied by 4% is equivalent to your yearly life costs.
- To personalize the process, determine the inputs (that affect income), and outputs (that affect spending) that

align with your values and test optimization strategies to maximize the results.

Disclaimer: I am not a certified financial advisor nor am I qualified to be yours. The information I share is merely to increase your awareness about money so you might have a transparent conversation with your accountant, tax advisor, or financial advisor whom you know, like, and trust.

Over the last five years, our yearly family expenses ranged between $72,000 and $90,000 for a family of five in Wisconsin. The buckets of housing, transportation, food, and personal expenses are fairly predictable and have been true to budget each month. The buckets of debt, savings, health, and discretionary expenses are more variable from month to month. Since I do not enjoy regularly tracking my spending, I do an audit every quarter to dive deep into actual expenses in one or two buckets. The process is "good enough" for me to feel confident in our numbers.

Making Money Fun

There is a fine line between confidence and arrogance. The narrative around money as a parent was to play it safe, and take the conservative route. What drew me to financial independence was I no longer had to design my life to fit my money; I could design my money to fit my life. If financial independence was the summit, I wanted to enjoy the journey testing our ideal life along the way.

We have an intention to keep our yearly budget to $75,000–$80,000 for our family of five. This requires us to be creative without sacrificing elements where we thrive. We highly value travel and adventure experiences informing spending decisions such as more travel, buying adventure equipment for birthday and holiday gifts, and minimizing the investments we make in other forms of entertainment throughout the year.

Do you remember that experiment to convince my husband traveling was worth $2,500 a year? The authentic experiences, fondly referred to as untourism, included the right elements of adventure, connection, and trying new things while traveling. The initial challenge of designing authentic experiences became more comfortable. While I wanted to travel more, I didn't want to increase our travel spending. The optimization strategy I landed on (thanks to Choose FI) was travel rewards. Through travel rewards, I could supplement our income using a different type of currency to support our travel expenses.

Travel Rewards

Travel rewards are a form of currency from travel brands. Consumers earn rewards through purchases, staying at hotels, flying with the airlines, or signing up for travel-branded credit cards. The financial habits I put in place in my money story gave me the confidence to step into the world of travel rewards. I signed up for two co-branded credit cards my first year. I tracked the timeline to meet the minimum spends with yearly planned purchases and attain large sign-up bonuses. I made sure to pay the credit card balance in full each month and used the credit card as needed to earn bonus points going forward. I had seen travel rewards work for young couples or singles, and I was determined to make it work for our family.

Travel rewards can be as complicated or as simple as you desire. I include a free Family Guide to Travel Rewards in the resource section of this book. I also offer travel rewards coaching to walk alongside families to design and implement a travel rewards strategy to achieve their travel goals. Travel rewards lessons (from me and others) are also featured on the Ordinary Sherpa podcast.

Our dream travel reward redemption thus far was flying five individuals from Milwaukee, WI, to Hawaii visiting three islands in three weeks. The total out of pocket cost for flights round trip was under $500. I walk through the detailed steps and exact amounts in episode 032 (ordinarysherpa.com/032) Using travel rewards still feels illegal, but it's not. We are playing by the rules established by the travel companies. Today, travel rewards account for over half of our travel spending.

Developing Systems

I took a training (Effective Edge through InteraWorks) that helped me create a system of what to do with all the information coming at me. My money story had nothing to do with money and everything to do with my mindset and creating systems for success. By unsubscribing and turning off notifications (on my calendar, email and phone), I had more space in my brain to multiply the aspects of my life that created value tenfold.

A second psychology trick was automating payments and savings. I call it a psychology trick because I lived in scarcity mode for so long that I feared not having enough. Since I spent so much time thinking and going through routine spending decisions, it took me a while to embrace automation. I tested automating savings first, and learned I rarely missed the automatic withdrawals, but I enjoyed the growing savings balance. The beautiful thing about automating savings was that I didn't see the checking account balance go up, which prevented me from becoming aloof with money. Clarity with our spending resulted in bills falling in line with our desired life costs.

Flipping the Script

Eventually, our money story flipped. We became good with money. When we began to drift in the comfort zone by making relatively unconscious spending and life decisions, we would challenge ourselves to reset. The appeal of simplicity was tugging for my attention, and I began to practice a quasi-minimalist approach. I maintained the value-adding thrifty features of my life while removing the excess clutter taking up physical and mental space.

I don't scrimp on a good coffee. My husband willingly spends money hunting and fishing each year. We prioritize activities like biking and skiing as a family. Our years practicing thrift allowed us to design a budget based on values, not consumer price tags. One of my proudest money moments was when the final expenses for our wedding came in under $7,500. We had the wedding of our dreams with 200 of our closest friends and family members. We balked at the average wedding costing $20,000 (in 2008). We proved them wrong with an elegant, simple, and economical wedding that many friends and family still talk about. We were clear about what we valued and put our own price tags on each item's worth.

Adventure FI

There are many on-ramps and off-ramps to and from financial independence. The why of our FI is to give ourselves permission to the live the life of our dreams, which includes an adventurous lifestyle with kids. You might sense by the examples in this book that our family has a deep desire to take a gap year to travel. Every year, we test aspects of our dream life to determine what to keep and what to leave behind. The $75,000–$80,000 we spend each year for our life includes "just enough" comforts for us to rest and retreat allowing us to invest in our dream lifestyle.

Manifesting our future life has made it easier to make decisions without complexity that can plague families long term. We have no desire to keep up with the Joneses. Our next ten years of family experiences have little to do with the size of our house or the things inside it.

Each of us has the autonomy to decide what we want our life to cost. The critical piece to all of this was not to simply consume information but to make progress—to take action just a little bit each day. With each step, I got a little closer to clarity. What does my life actually cost? How do I create space between my income and expenses? And my favorite: It's December 2030 (choose a date five years from now). You are looking back at the last five years of your life. What does it feel like?

Money is a tool. Like any other tool, it will not build the solution. We decide what we want to do with the money. It doesn't determine anything about us. Anytime I see stories about "the average cost of _____" (fill in the blank: housing, college, vacation, living), I roll my eyes and acknowledge, "We aren't average!" We have designed our life based on the values we uphold and spend our money accordingly. In the next section, I'll walk through how we make decisions.

Key Takeaways

The beautiful thing about money is that it's basic math, and there is always an answer. Here are some questions to consider from this chapter:

- How much does your life actually cost? When we know the numbers we are working with, we can figure out what we need and define how to get there.
- Worry magnifies problems. How much do you think it cost me in my time and energy currency for the $600 overdraft expenses?
- There are three money variables you can influence: income, expenses, and the gap from the difference. Could you spend less in certain areas? Could you create revenue in other areas? How could you optimize your life to cost less overall?
- What optimization strategies exist to reduce spending in your current spending categories?
- When making financial decisions in relationships, what is the dollar amount you are comfortable with your partner transacting without your consent?
- Why do you say no? The twenty-four-hour rule gave both parties time between the stimulus and the response. Increasing the time between the thought to the purchase decisions allows both parties to process their thoughts.
- It's five years from today. You are looking back at the last five years of your life. What does it feel like?

Making Decisions

*"Never allow waiting to become a habit. Love your
dreams and take risks. Life is happening now."*
—Paulo Coelho

Have you ever hung out with a group of people trying to make a decision, and everyone is lukewarm or indifferent? Making decisions can be the hardest part of this guide because we are so wired to want to make the *right* decision. According to researchers at Cornell University, the average adult makes 35,000 decisions per day.[14] Each decision has varying degrees of benefits and consequences that can lead to burnout and overwhelm. You likely have heard of FOMO, a term coined by Pat McGinnis. He now speaks of a growing debilitating sister, FOBO, or Fear of a Better Option. We don't make decisions because we are trying to make the *right* decision, knowing there might be a better option out there.

Thinking vs. Feeling

We live in a complex society. Complex issues and problems are usually filled with layers of information and considerations. Regardless, if we are in business or nonprofit work, the normal way we are taught to solve problems is with data, logic, and best practices, usually biased with our own ideas, perspectives, and experiences. I refer to this category of information and research as head data.

Head data is thinking our way through a problem. However, if we were to spend time falling in love with the problem and digging deep into our empathy ethos, we could get more in-tune with the feelings and intuition side of the data equation. Feeling data is often overlooked or silenced in problem-solving, yet it leads to transformational change by getting real and digging into understanding our stories, perspectives, and experiences. If we give this heart-based data the same weight as head-based data, we can move forward with greater clarity, intention, and purpose.

Assigning Value

I noticed my life offered greater focus and value after the introduction of minimalism concepts. Joshua Fields Millburn and Ryan Nicodemus of *The Minimalists* describe minimalism as "a lifestyle that helps people question what things add value to their lives. By clearing the clutter from life's path, we can all make room for the most important aspects of life: health, relationships, passion, growth, and contribution."[15] While many might understand minimalism to suggest the removal of clutter in their lives, I like to think of it more as clarity on what you value. I first practiced minimalism by starting with money.

I wanted to focus on my mindless spending and clarify what led to unplanned expenses. Although being thrifty is part of my persona, I realized I was addicted to the emotional high of a sale. I would get enamored by the act of buying something cheap even if it wasn't necessary. I also noticed emotional spends while on a high, like vacation, where I would spend way more money than I normally would, for the YOLO effect. Through my Joy Audit, I realized the amount of money I spent on an experience was not synonymous with the amount of joy I felt. The emotional high was also the cost of escape.

In many cases, the dopamine hit of buying something different or buying something cheap was short-lived. High-impact joy comes from memorable or share-worthy experiences. I couldn't simply chase joy with a dopamine hit. I needed to learn and feel my way through the phase of defining what I valued and what the other members of my family valued. I soon learned to use money to *reinforce* the joy, and stopped expecting money to *create* joy.

While minimalism means different things to different people, for me, it simplifies the options and aligns the greatest potential for impact. If I have too many material or emotions options, making a decision gets hard. Let's take the concept of minimalism and apply it to our thoughts.

Fewer Options, Greater Value

For starters, cut the number of decisions in half immediately and then limit your options. One of my favorite things to do is grocery shop. (Yes, I am 100% serious!). It is the one challenge from my thrifty days that I continue to enjoy. For a family of five, I try to keep our food budget around $600 a month. For a long time, I would make my grocery list, then look through the advertisements to find the best price, and then look to see if there were coupons. In the end, grocery shopping became work. Now my approach is much simpler. I make the grocery list based on what meals people value. That might mean that either a) all of us like the meal and will find great satisfaction, b) it will have a greater impact on one of the family members and create a better experience for that person, or c) It will create a new experience for all of us through a new or different recipe.

Freezer real estate is at a premium in our house, so I try to make sure whatever freezer items I purchase will have the best impact on my family. I don't chase sales anymore. I seldom clip coupons, yet we still spend the same or less. The savings come from limiting the number of choices and crowdsourcing the high-value items. I only look at the prices of two or three items as opposed to the entire department so I won't be paralyzed by a decision overload.

Boundaries and Experiences

I have become so clear on the grocery list that there is very little energy required. I now invite one of our three children to go grocery shopping with me. I empower them to make decisions on several items they find value in, which doubles as a fun connection opportunity. By putting boundaries around a decision, it shifts from overwhelm to a fun experience for independence and connection. I am using the grocery shopping since it is a practical example, however, crafting clarity around three or four high-value items and setting boundaries is a practice relevant to many other life adventures. (I'll share a few adventure examples in the Play Wildly section).

If we can clarify what we value, we can immediately divide the number of decisions (35,000 a day) in half or maybe even reduce them by 75%. Why? Because we don't really care about those decisions. Does it matter if I eat cereal or eggs for breakfast? Wear red or black? There are so many decisions that have us stuck spending time and energy on things when the result will have minimal, if any, impact on our future. If we focus on the decisions that are important, we can reduce the overall strain on our brains.

Notice-Choose-Act

When I'm stuck in a swirling state of indecisions, I use the Notice-Choose-Act sequence. **Notice** what is possible, **choose** what serves us (and what doesn't), and **act** on that choice. Many people notice things in life they don't like; they are the complainers. A surprising number of people forget they have the power to choose the next step.

People who choose something different from the status quo often get stuck in the choose mode. They have the idea but sit on it. The most critical step is taking action, which often requires courage.

When I stepped into an executive role, I quickly learned I needed to make decisions sometimes with only 60% of the information. If I waited to gather 100% of the information to make the right decision, it would not be as impactful. Instead, I had to navigate which decisions to seek input on and which decisions I should make with the information I had. When I realized the bulk of my decisions in life came down to those three steps—notice, choose, act—the world opened up to me.

Now I make it a point to take action on three things every single day. By focusing on three things, the probability of success is higher. I include an action item on the list each day to put a deposit in my energy bank account—something that would refresh and give me energy.

Optimizing Family Experiences without Sacrificing Value

Let's put this into adventure context. My family wanted to go skiing out west. Since there are 196 ski hills to choose from, this is the framework I used to design our ideal family ski experience.

- What is the purpose, intention, or goal for the experience?

- What will create value?
- How can we leverage our network and optimize for value?
- What resources do we already have?

1. Purpose

What is the ideal experience you want to create? I began with what is valued most—an affordable family skiing experience. I researched "family friendly ski resorts." Since we are from the Midwest, we were not looking for the five-star experience; we were simply looking for a different experience. I also looked into which ski resorts participated in passport programs to expose 4th—6th graders.

What are the cheapest routes to get there? Notice we haven't decided on our destination yet. I let fare sales and schedules decide our ultimate route. From the list of ski passport programs, I selected airports in Albuquerque, Denver, Boise, and Salt Lake City to look into. Because my husband and I had a companion pass, travel rewards, and a travel voucher to use on Southwest Airlines, I started with their Low Fare flight calendar. We selected the dates and location based on the price. A round trip flight for one person was $147.96 to Denver.

Three tickets were covered by the travel voucher and travel rewards, and our two sons fly free as our designated companions. The cost for the five of us was $11.20 to cover security fees (not redeemable through points). Southwest would also be ideal since two bags fly free, and our ski gear would need to be checked luggage. (If you want to learn more about travel rewards being a tool in designing your life of adventure, make sure to check out the resources section for a free download.)

2. Leverage

Get recommendations from your network. I highly value learning from others and garnering local experiences. After selecting Colorado as our location, I crowdsourced ratings and insights to inform our decisions. I have family near Estes Park, Colorado, and while they don't ski, they know which options are close. I am a member of a Ski Moms Fun Facebook group. I listed the 21 ski resorts included in the Colorado ski passport program for grades 4–6 and asked the group to choose their top four family-friendly resorts with great skiing.

Since I value a local "untourist" experience at less-crowded locations, I took the top five to ten recommendations and looked at aggregator sites like TripAdvisor or Google Travel to read the reviews. The locations at the top of the page often have marketing budgets, but I prefer smaller businesses and local favorites, so I scrolled to the middle of the page.

Optimize the details. I took all the recommendations, dug into lodging options, explored trail maps, and reviewed lift ticket prices. We checked out lodging and car rental options through the Chase Ultimate Rewards (travel rewards currency) portal to see how else we could optimize our budget with rewards. Airbnb and Turo were still ideal for our family from the cost and amenities perspective. The high-value items were a bed for everyone to sleep in, a convenient way to store and transport our ski equipment, a kitchen to prepare meals, and proximity to skiing to ideally get out for our first run and come back for lunch midday.

3. Already Have

Reuse what works, and value what's important. Skiing is a sport that requires significant cold weather gear and equipment that can be expensive. Since we value family-friendly lifestyle activities, we invested in skiing equipment to make the adventure desirable for everyone. We buy all equipment used and in gender-neutral colors to make use of hand-me-downs and avoid the costs of repeatedly renting equipment. I also buy high-quality ski jackets and snow pants at the local skier's outlet, rummage sales, or used-gear places.

I ended up planning the bulk of this trip in less than six hours. In the end, our stay was at a 4.8-Star resort. It was a high-joy experience with challenging but fun ski conditions. The added bonus was that it doubled as one of the family experience gifts for Christmas. Our total expense of $1,517.63 is still a small portion of the $5,980.58 average cost of a family ski weekend.[16]

Creating a practice of reducing the options, prioritizing action over perfection, and focusing on what we value are the three steps we use to reduce the noise. We spend less time stressing about the decision-making process.

Minimalism has been a great framework to help me reduce the noise and get clear on what I value. I have no shame in unsubscribing; my FOMO rating has drastically decreased in the past three years. (If I do fall prey to FOMO, the daily brain dump helps me move forward. It might mean saving that idea for a someday/maybe list, then revisiting the list once a year to see if it's still relevant or if I need to eliminate it altogether). We'll dive deeper into feeling based decision-making in the next chapter.

Key Takeaways

Quiet the noise by reducing the number of decisions you make. Here are key questions and action steps from this chapter:

- Which is more difficult for you to work through, FOMO (fear of missing out) or FOBO (fear of a better option)?
- Use money to *reinforce* joy, and do not expect money to *create* joy.
- On average we make 35,000 decisions a day. How can you eliminate 90% of decisions that have little value on the overall impact of your life?
- Notice-Choose-Act: Aim for action. Even small actions every day lead to big results over time.
- Crowdsource the choices based on high-value options.
- When designing an experience, consider:
- What is the purpose, intention, or goal for the experience?
- What will create value?
- How can we leverage our network and optimize for value?
- What resources do we already have?

Thinking with Your Heart

"Travel is not a rational activity. It makes no sense to squeeze yourself into an alleged seat only to be hurled at frightening speed to a distant place where you don't speak the language or know the customs. All at great expense. If we stopped to do the cost-benefit analysis, we'd never go anywhere. And yet we do."
—Eric Weiner

I would consider the practice of minimizing the number of decisions a tactical approach. Another approach is recognizing the feelings we attach to decisions. The bulk of my life was spent trying to find the right answer, yet 90% of the decisions in my life didn't *have* a right answer. Looking back the motivator for these decisions came from feelings of guilt, anxiousness, or frustration.

The Merit of Feelings

Our thoughts control our feelings. Our feelings add a considerable amount of time and energy to the equation, sometimes leading us to do nothing. When we put too much time and energy into thinking about or analyzing something, we can do more harm than good.

I thought my head did the thinking and my heart did the feeling. Our feelings might also be characterized as our heart, our gut, or our intuition. One of the greatest sources of data is our feelings. When I ignore my gut, my head gets confused. I am thrust into the world of overthinking. As a Western society, we have placed greater emphasis on thinking our way through a problem. It makes logical sense when we explain our answer. Many decisions don't have a correct answer. Solving the problem with logic uses only one tool. Even running a tally on the pros and cons can prove to be nebulous.

Past Experiences

I have been on a journey to unlearn some of what I thought to be true. One example of thinking with our heart is recognizing that our past experiences are not definitive predictors of our future.

Past experiences become loud voices establishing themselves as benchmarks in our thoughts. The voice inside our head tends to be strong. Have you ever experienced when loud voices seem to take over? Loud voices are not smarter or better; they are simply louder and sometimes more annoying.

Having facilitated countless meetings and strategy sessions, I know how hard it is to draw out the quieter voices. It requires intentionality to turn down the noise stealing the attention.

I like the imagery of our thoughts (our head) being the loud noise and our feelings (our hearts) being the quiet inner voice. We have to quiet the background noise so we can hear our heart, gut, or intuition. When our worlds are filled with noise, we have to combat it with stillness. It's an extremely challenging practice; however, it has never failed me.

Thinking with Your Heart

Thinking with your heart transforms problem-solving. Every. Single. Time. I find clarity in stillness. When faced with a problem to solve, my brain instinctively begins with ideas and thoughts. One of the most transformative problem-solving lessons I've learned was to start with empathy and allow feelings to have priority. A critical skill when designing experiences is to empathize with recipients. Building our capacity to listen and feel through the experience by asking questions. If I begin with thinking, I add my biased perspective to a problem that hasn't been clearly defined.

Some questions I like to ask are: Tell me about the best part of being (their age/grade) today? If you could choose to spend your day doing anything you want, what would the day look like? Describe a scary/hilarious experience you've had. These invitations provide gifts in the form of eliciting their stories. Stories create context and connection.

The art of underthinking requires less thinking and more doing. When you manifest a vision about the future where you feel scared and excited, it's usually a good sign. It's easy to get stuck there, dreaming and thinking. Loud voices are often rooted in negative feelings and experiences. Thinking recycles those negative experiences, whereas action breeds different results.

Favoring Action

In research and development, there is a process known as A/B testing. A/B testing is trying Option A and Option B with only one variable changed then studying which option performs better. I apply A/B testing encourages taking action using two similar but different options and gathering feedback from customers, family, friends—whomever you want to receive feedback from. At some point, the only way to make progress is to lean into action.

Planning and testing yield different outcomes. Testing a decisions provides richer information than a plan with each step predicted. In the family ski experience (referenced in the previous chapter) the planning (thinking) process would be to choose a destination, book a flight, confirm accommodations and then decide the ski resort based on how many ads I see when searching online. The testing (feeling) process, reinforces what people value most. By prioritizing how people feel leads to more enriching experiences based on peoples values. Thinking with your heart favors testing, action and feedback.

Intention-Setting

Lifestyle Design is a method of continuously asking yourself questions, testing the response, and collecting feedback. Once I was asked to reflect on this scenario:

It's ten years from now, and you are looking back at your life.

- What do you want to feel?
- What are you proudest of?

My answer was, "Every day felt like vacation." I am a travel superfan. Before I am home from one vacation, I am already planning the next one. As I grew in life, the travels changed but never stopped. When the statement "Every day felt like a vacation" came, I immediately imagined taking a year off to travel the world. I noticed the feeling in my body was ease and joy.

Seconds later, my brain executed a hard stop and slammed reality in my face. All the reasons that dream wouldn't become a reality came rushing to the forefront of my mind. Rather than listening to those rational thoughts, I decided to let my feelings be heard. *Thinking with your heart allows feelings to have a voice.*

How Might We...

I compiled a "How might we... " list, writing down every way that could come true. Some simple reflections and deeper questions were revealed, offering greater clarity. These were some of the questions, along with their answers:

- What does a vacation feel like? My response was, "together having fun as a family exploring something new and different without the distractions and expectations of daily life, work, and school. We could just be together, laughing, exploring, and curious about the world."
- How might I create that experience at home? This question hit me in the face. I had been so focused on escaping reality I never thought to make experiences at home mimic a vacation. "We could turn off the screens. We could have a *no responsibility day of the week*. We could do simple adventures nearby that we have never experienced before. We could turn a space in our home into a retreat space. We could sleep in the camper and pretend we were camping." The dam of possibilities was opened, and my initial fear and anger were bowled over with joy and possibilities.

Without changing my reflection statement, I could have simple and authentic vacation experiences tomorrow *and* continue working toward a full-blown vacation lifestyle. I have since swapped the word *vacation* to *adventurous* to better align with my intentions. *Every day feels adventurous.*

Through the process of simple and authentic experiences, I realized society attaches spending and luxury to the word *vacation*, whereas *adventure* brought out more of a curious and playful mindset. Today, our entire family has embraced an adventure lifestyle. Given the definition of adventure is to have a new, uncomfortable experience, we are practicing every day to get better at trying new things, getting curious about things we aren't familiar with. *Thinking with your heart encourages curiosity.*

Exposure Therapy*

*Disclaimer, I am not skilled in exposure therapy as a practice, which is why I feel compelled to use the term as a slang definition in italics. A friend and I began using this phrase, trying to expose our spouses to different ideas or ways to live our lives outside the conventional nine-to-five.

The continuous testing offers benefits I like to call a *no-thank-you try* and *exposure therapy. Exposure therapy* introduces you to things you didn't know existed or didn't consider as options. Until we rented the RV in 2020, I never would have considered living on the road in an RV for a year. It was my first *exposure therapy* to this type of experience. Recognizing the options, driven by feelings and intuition, is a critical step in moving beyond normal.

I have always dreamed of taking a year off and traveling the world. I didn't know what that would be like or when it would happen; it just seemed to be this elusive thing that I would get excited about. In 2020, when all our travel was canceled, and I was in dire need of a different experience, we rented an RV that had all the things to be self-contained for a significant amount of time.

Prior to 2020, I was opposed to purchasing a camper. In fact, I was quite emphatic about it. I wanted to jump on planes and stay in houses around the world. I had only been exposed to people who parked their RV in a permanent campsite and treated it like their cabin with several hundred other people nearby. To me, an RV was an anchor that limited travel to nearby locations.

Testing the RV experience gave me a completely different perspective of RV life I never imagined. It gave us freedom and control (how is that for an oxymoron) to design our travel experience however we wanted. We knew what to expect each night. We had a bathroom and kitchen everywhere we went. There were still some inconveniences involved in driving a twenty-six-foot vehicle, but for the most part, we weren't beholden to any location or defined itinerary. What started as a dire need to travel opened our eyes to a delightful and fulfilling RV experience. *Thinking with your heart opens doors you thought were closed.*

Learning by Doing

That test led to more testing. Could we live together in a camper for longer than two weeks? How often did we need to change locations? Could I still work remotely while being on the road? Each question led to a new test, learning by doing. Rather than thinking and trying to read, listen, and study our way to a decision, we simply kept doing tests to see what the outcome was. *Thinking with your heart allows you to change course even if you don't have all the answers.*

I might be one of the 7% of people who actually loves their job. I'm well-compensated, and the risk of leaving sends anxiety through my body. What if I am not able to find another job like this? (PS: This is scarcity mindset). On the flip side, my kids are six, nine, and eleven. They are ages where a season is about to expire.

I don't have all the answers, and there is a significant amount of energy currency being spent throughout this decision-making process. However, *exposure therapy* to RV life demonstrated we all genuinely enjoy life on the road, experiencing different places, meeting new people, or reconnecting with friends and family from afar. When we embraced and accepted the worst-case scenarios, they were all manageable risks. We continue to learn there are very few decisions in life that are permanent. The *exposure therapy* to RV life allowed us to see what was possible outside our zone of awareness. *Thinking with your heart encourages exposure to new experiences*

No-Thank-You Try

Fun fact. Did you know kids need to taste things roughly ten times before they know if they like the food?[17] Even then, what we like is constantly changing and evolving. Therefore, the *no-thank-you try* is an attempt to taste or try something. We aren't committing to an entire serving; we are simply taking a bite or dipping our toe in and deciding whether we want to go further. When we have big crazy ideas, we try to create a *no-thank-you try* experience to learn from, iterate, and try again.

Here are some of the *no-thank-you try* experiments we have done in the last couple of years:

1. Crazy Idea: My five-year-old wants us to buy him a dirt bike. In fairness, my husband and older son are also gearheads. His relentless asking and urging led us to take action with a *no-thank-you try.* We knew a family with kids our age who race dirt bikes. We told them about our son's desire to ride dirt bikes and requested a schedule to attend one of their races. We took the RV and camped with them the night before so the kids could see the gear, the setup, and take a few rides on the dirt bike. My son realized how hard (and a bit scary) it was to ride the bike on the dirt track. We also saw how they spent many of their summer weekends. We witnessed things go wrong and how tricky it was to race on trails. Does my son still want a dirt bike? Yes. However, we can have practical conversations about what that would mean for the entire family and what we wouldn't be able to do in the summer if we got a dirt bike. Instead, we agreed to invest a little more in their mountain bikes, offering a bit more adventurous experience. We also could easily travel with our mountain bikes.

2. Crazy Idea: Spontaneous boys' night. The older kids were invited to sleep over at a friend's house. My youngest wasn't at the stage in friendships where sleepovers were a thing. He was completely crushed and asked if he and dad could go camping in the RV. Within thirty minutes from our house is a state park campground with mountain bike trails and a lake for fishing and swimming. We have an RV. We booked a spot at 7 p.m., gathered a few items, and off they went. We can create one-on-one experiences or spontaneous adventures with less than an hour of planning.

3. Crazy Idea: Can we balance work and school life while adventuring? In March of 2021, we found an RV to purchase in Florida. We made the one-way flight arrangements. My husband only had one personal day, so he had to fly back to work for a few days and meet back up with us for his scheduled spring break. I was alone with three kids, a brand-new RV, and still needed to work. For three days, I woke up at 5:30 a.m. and immediately got to work. The kids woke up on their schedule, ate breakfast, and settled into their schoolwork until around 10 a.m. Then they would go outside to play. At 11:30, I took a break from work (with six hours in), had lunch with the kids, and made plans for afternoon adventures. On those three days, I used two hours of Paid Time Off so I could be present with the kids. We rode bikes, we walked to the beach, and we played games. It was the most laid back and connected I felt as a family in a long time. We did simple things while still adventuring in our local area. I would later try working a couple of days in the RV while my husband was there to help with the kids and decided that eight hours per day, or full-time work, was much harder. It felt like I was missing out on all the adventures. Full-time work while adventuring did not seem sustainable.

Those *no-thank-you tries* at first impulse would likely have resulted in a "no" response. By embracing a mini-experiment, I could test bits and pieces to see what was worth keeping and what could be left behind. The other benefit of a *no-thank-you try* is everyone was involved in the decision, as opposed to Mom and Dad making the decision. The kids still experienced it and saw the joys and struggles of trying. One key aspect is remembering we may need ten tries to determine whether we actually like something. Even when we have strong feelings on our first *no-thank-you try*, having a few more "tastes" of an idea is good practice before making the official decision if necessary. *Thinking with our heart allows us to try something without future commitment.*

Beyond Normal

We grow up with stories and experiences relative to the people and places in our lives. We frame our beliefs based on a series of experiences, and somehow, over time, these thoughts, beliefs, and experiences become our norms. Until we are exposed to a different thought, a different idea, or a different way, we tend to fall back on our norms.

As someone who grew up with two working parents outside the home at conventional nine-to-five jobs, the idea of being an entrepreneur took some *exposure therapy*. I had side hustles for most of my life. I always considered it just that: a side thing. It took me interacting and connecting with others doing this full-time and thriving for me to embrace entrepreneurship as a potential option.

Even more radical was the idea that we could save over 50% of our income and use different investment strategies to achieve financial independence at an age much earlier than many. Essentially, we could achieve the amount of assets required to retire and have enough to live the rest of our lives by a simple math formula. We have complete control over how much we spend each year and what we want our life to look like.

Exposure to financial independence completely changed my world. I hit a point in my life when I thought the next milestone would be retiring in thirty-plus years. *Exposure therapy* can be both freeing and terrifying because you realize nothing in this world is binary. Rather, it is a field of potential, and the horizon is wide open with possibilities. *Thinking with your heart allows for nonbinary choices.*

Seeking Familiarity

Recognizing potential options is a critical step in moving beyond normal. Our brain is designed to see opportunities we are exposed to more regularly. This "part of our brain cells (is) called the reticular activating system. It's our program to seek similarity."[18] We look for things that are familiar and similar.

Ever take a car for a test drive and then weeks later see that car everywhere? That is our brain trying to associate with things that are familiar to us. Are you surrounded by bad news, and suddenly the world feels like it's falling apart? There is significant psychology suggesting we find comfort in things we are familiar with.

Exposure therapy helped me see blind spots and led me to seek out people who might have similar interests yet have completely different experiences than me. It also led me to learn and grow in the dimensions of my life that were intriguing, but I had little experience. If we hang out with people who haven't been exposed to a different lifestyle or idea, it's not normal to them. Keep that in mind as you form your tribe.

Many people will look at a scenario and make decisions based on their strengths, often rooted in their comfort zone. Our natural tendencies (based on StrengthFinders, Disc, Meyers Briggs profile, or Enneagram) might lead us down a predictable path. Some of my checkpoints for these big decisions for the crossroads in life are:

- What is the risk vs. reward?
- What will I regret more later (doing it or not doing it)?
- If the worst-case scenario happens, what does that mean for me/us?
- Why am I drawn to this?
- Does this align with what I value and believe in? (Is it a hell *yes*?)

I'd encourage you to think about your questions. What are the gut checks you already do when you make big decisions in life? How could you test the decision in the simplest format?

In the next chapter, we will discuss how to work with or against the pull of the downstream affect.

Key Takeaways

There are very few decisions in life that are permanent. When we think with our hearts, we allow ourselves to feel our way through decisions. These principles are designed to support deeper exploration:

- Thinking with your heart allows for nonbinary choices.
- Thinking with our heart allows us to try something without future commitment.

- Thinking with your heart encourages exposure to new experiences.
- Thinking with your heart allows you to change course even if you don't have all the answers.
- Thinking with your heart opens doors you thought were closed.
- Thinking with your heart encourages curiosity.
- Thinking with your heart allows feelings to have a voice.
- Thinking with your Heart Transforms Problem-Solving.

The Current of Normal

"If you are always trying to be normal, you will never know how amazing you can be."
—Maya Angelou

I recall an experience at eighteen years old when a friend and I decided to go white water rafting. It was just the two of us, no guide, no experience, just a raft, some paddles, and life jackets with three to four hours of an unknown adventure ahead of us. We launched from a secluded area in the wilderness. The river was calm—almost uncomfortably calm, and I thought perhaps we had made the wrong decision. I was mentally prepared for rapids and hard work, but it was really boring!

Sometimes, we overlook the beauty of calmness, wishing and waiting for the exciting part. As in life, the ordinary everyday routines are easy to overlook—easy to crave something bigger, something more exciting. When we fail to recognize the calm, we look past the lessons life is trying to prepare us for. The calm was my opportunity to learn how to maneuver the raft and practice things that would be much harder to learn in turbulent waters. When the rapids arrived, I quickly realized I wasn't prepared. Not only were we dodging rocks, but we were also fighting the pull of the current in directions that didn't align with our intentions. While current is most often recognized as an external force pulling downstream, it can also be an internal force—with thoughts and feelings drawing our energy downstream.

The Joy of Calm

I woke up one Saturday morning in the recliner with a gentle rub on my shoulder. Dancing flames filled the fireplace, smothered in a velvet blanket and earbuds from my recent guided meditation still snug in my ears. I emerged from rest to see my oldest son at my side. It was a moment of calm.

My mind and body had been on perpetual overdrive. This was the first time in weeks I could remember feeling calm. *Honor it, savor it, welcome it,* a quiet voice within me whispered. Busyness and productivity were downstream currents, the narrative and social phenomenon that framed my definition of *normal.*

It almost felt like a competition among friends and family of who was busier. Taking a break had long looked like an escape. Throughout my life, I would get through the grind and hit the deadline only to be completely exhausted. My natural cure was to travel or attend a social gathering to numb the feeling of responsibility. While travel has long been my drug of choice, it isn't treatment. In the words of Matt Kepnes (a.k.a. Nomadic Matt), "travel doesn't let you escape your past. Your demons will always find some space in the bottom of your backpack."

Joy is not a destination; not a rung on the ladder. Joy is a sense of being, an alignment with your purpose, a keen awareness of all that surrounds you. Joy was waking up that Saturday morning with a sense of calm. Over the course of thirty minutes, all the kids walked up to the recliner I was sitting in with a welcome embrace, a "snugglefest" as we like to call them, each child having a unique way to express their love.

The snow fell in rhythm to the piano music. The house was disheveled, reflecting playful times. The kids were likely wearing yesterday's clothes, and I'm sure morning breath permeated from my pores. Yet by my definition, it was a perfect moment.

The status quo of normal life can be synonymous with the downstream current. We drift easily from one place to the next without much thought, planning, or strain. In order to find moments of calm and stillness we might need to drop anchor or work against the current to get to shore.

External Forces

When you drop anchor or attempt to dock, you immediately feel the external forces of current working against you. Sometimes it's easier to float with the current than to intentionally pause or working upstream. One might wish stillness is like pressing pause on a movie. When I try to pause life, it seems the world around me speeds up.

Mindfulness practices were my attempt to pause. I hoped my brain and everything around me would stop; quite the opposite happened. I noticed every noise, every distraction. My thoughts continued racing and wandering. For me, mindfulness was like trying to paddle our raft out of the rapids toward shore. The current is strongest in the deepest part of the river. As you get closer to the shore, the pull is weaker. It's easier to navigate life at slower speeds.

Paddling Downstream

Each season on the river is different. If the water is high, the current is fast, and there is less paddling required. If the water is low, the current is slower, and there are more logs and snags to avoid or work through. Our family friends regularly take a paddle down the river. We joined them for one trip for a convoy of two canoes and four kayaks hauling four adults and five kids (ages five to eleven). We allow the kids to either kayak or simply ride in the canoe if they want.

My five-year-old was determined to kayak. We tied his kayak to another adult's kayak to make it a little easier for him to navigate, still giving him some independence, and easing my momma mind. The river was low, meaning the current wasn't scary fast but high enough to easily navigate many of the logs and rocks.

In one section, there was a little rapids area with lots of rocks to navigate. A kayak got stuck on a rock, which caused the other kayaks to jam up on the rocks as well. My five-year-old saw that he was stuck, and suddenly the current coming at him seemed really fast and scary. The current was there all along, but he didn't notice it nor was he afraid of it until he got stuck.

Getting Stuck

When we get hung up on something, it can feel like the entire world is caving in on us. My five-year-old pleaded to be rescued. In that instance, we needed to get out of the boats to reposition our kayaks to point back downstream. When I am stuck, overwhelmed, or scared, someone always shows up and offers to help. Different people have different experiences and skills and can open our world to other ways.

Have you ever been stuck on the water? It can be the most relaxing and terrifying thing ever. The harder you try and the more energy you exert, the deeper you get stuck. There will be times in life when working harder actually creates more harm than good. You realize things are outside your control and submit to the world around you. The moment of awakening is when you realize you must submit to the universe and ask for help. The only way out is to receive the generosity and connection of others.

People around You

Sometimes, the current of normal has little to do with where we are in life, rather who we are surrounded by. I was a first-generation college student. It didn't seem like that big of a deal to me until my sophomore year of college. I was taking a twenty-four credit course load, working two part-time jobs, and competing on the college track team.

The difference between college and high school was noticeable for me. I didn't struggle much in high school with academics. I wasn't the valedictorian but received mostly A's and B's without much struggle. I was a three-sport athlete, held many leadership positions, and still worked part-time. Achieving was relatively easy. I assumed college would be more of the same.

College came with much more rigor. The stakes seemed higher, and I was investing so much money to attain the status of having a degree. The people around me in college had similar goals and aspirations creating a swell of people headed in similar directions, which can create quite a force to work against. That groundswell in college was achievement. While I didn't intentionally work against it, it consumed me.

Different Boats

One week, my mom had been trying to get in touch with me (before the era of cell phones). I left my dorm each morning at 7:30 a.m. for class and often didn't return for more than a few minutes until 11 p.m. or later. My mom had no idea of the rigor of my schedule and was quite upset with me for not calling her back. Each night, I got the message and thought, *I can't call now; she'll be in bed.*

She was extremely upset when I finally called her a few days later. I tried to explain, but it didn't really matter because she didn't understand what my days were like. She had good reason for being upset with me, too. My grandma had cancer. Mom didn't want to leave that news on voice mail, and to her, I seemed to be uninterested in returning her call.

We were both at a point in our lives where we couldn't relate to the current of the other person's daily flow. The things that were filling our time, stealing our energy, and consuming our resources were different. We were simply in different boats.

When the people we know, love, and trust are in different boats, it can be scary or confusing. We question where we are headed or if we are doing the right thing. How do we move forward while not abandoning those from our past? The expectations from others, without a self-check, can pull us out of alignment, especially if those expectations do not align with our needs, wants, and desires.

Finding a Tribe

One of the most challenging aspects of this entire journey was finding my tribe. A tribe can refer to a group of people who share similar culture, beliefs, and religion. As Seth Godin refers to the tribe concept in his book *Tribes*, "A tribe is a group of people connected to one another, connected to a leader, and connected to an idea." Find people with whom you feel connected and who believe in and support your ideas.

A quote that keeps my tribe in check is, "If you look at the people in your circle, and you don't get inspired, then you don't have a circle, you have a cage." We need people in our life that challenge us, support us, and inspire us—even if we are in different boats. As life evolves, we develop a new and improved idea of what this life can be. There will be some people who simply don't get it. As Jillian Johnsrud might say, "They don't see the vision you have for your life."

Fork in the Stream

I noticed a few key transition points in life—single to married, no kids to kids when we straddle the line with our friends, trying to navigate what to do with whom. Being married with kids brought with it a different set of responsibilities and expectations. I know some felt left behind, and others opted out of having screaming babies. Moments like these exemplify when you might be in different boats from others in your life.

It's easy to think we have to choose. Life is not about making binary choices. There are many ways to approach relationships at a confluence. It's not as simple as "Should I stay or should I go." Not all paths emanate from a definitive fork, continuing in different directions. I have been on several paddles where you can go left or right at the fork, and both meet back up downstream. I am finding that some of our friends and family are drawn to a different current. It doesn't mean I let them drown. Nor does it mean everyone needs rescuing from their own life.

Noticing the different currents at play in our life is like an awakening. When I notice different currents, I feel both energized and overwhelmed, not sure which way to go. I start swirling in all the new ideas and collect gurus to help me navigate this current. *I'm out too far, and the current is too fast.*

Reprieve

I am learning that when things feel like they are swirling, I either need to drop anchor or head to shore. The current is always calmer in shallow waters. When we are working so hard and our minds are racing, it is hard to hear our inner voice. Likewise, it's hard to notice different currents when we are stuck in the middle of one. The shore can allow a reprieve into our comfort zones to allow us to slow down and catch our breath.

When we return home from traveling, the comforts of home offer a sense of awe. There is also a twenty-four- to forty-eight-hour period of awareness and wonder that keeps us mindful of the current pulling us "back to normal" and often a busy life. We come back home to be surrounded by people who didn't share the same travel experience with us.

Connecting with Others

Currents tugging at many adults are status, ideology, money, or things. Those are strong currents. For us to resist the pull, we needed to connect with others who valued adventure. We sought families who weren't motivated purely by career and money goals. We noticed others who were trying new things and embracing change around them.

Once I embraced the unique and weird things about myself and our family, I realized they are superpowers not deficiencies. I no longer needed to fit in and compare myself to the status quo. I was creating a new current and attracting a new tribe. I didn't feel compelled to chase what others had. It didn't feel rejected or left out. I knew what was right for us and let others follow their own current.

Inviting Others In

Sometimes, we will be curious about others' currents, and sometimes others will be curious about our current. The invitation is with questions. If I ask questions about their life, their intentions, and realize they aren't on the same current as I, we simply enjoy our time together and move on. There is no need to rescue them or convince them to get out of the current that is sucking them downstream. They aren't flailing. They aren't asking for help, no need to throw the life ring in their direction.

If no one asks questions about the currents of my life, they aren't interested. The chapters of this book are based on sixteen questions I fielded from parents wanting to live an adventurous life. A key lesson in building a tribe of adventurous friends is to ask questions of those you might be admiring near or far. A simple question to ask them is "How can I help?" The people in your tribe represent relationships that have been built. How can I put myself in close proximity to others doing adventurous things? I might explore activities, meet ups, memberships, or even virtual spaces to get to know others with shared interests. Am I asking questions? How am I offering to help?

Be Where Your Feet Are

When designing a less-traditional or adventurous lifestyle, we often have to work against the current. We are paddling upstream, and there are stages when doubt will creep in, fear fills our body, our safety instincts are on high alert. Our ability to overcome the pull wears down our stamina. Our energy currency can easily be depleted. Ideally, we practice dropping anchor or docking when the current is not strong.

Normal is the current of an ordinary life. Without intentional actions, we will drift downstream, and thirty years will pass. Floating on the river, life seems easy, relaxing, and serene. When you stand up on the bed of the river, you can feel the force of the current tugging at your ankles. That is the current of normal.

I use the phrase "be where your feet are" as a grounding practice to focus on where you physically are right now. Get out of your head, take your life off drift, and just notice what is happening in front of you. This is the life you want to be present for. *Wishing away the calm* is my trigger or a checkpoint to slow down and take note. Notice the calm, embrace the calm, and practice life when it's slow.

Near the very end of our exhausting and eventful whitewater rafting trip, there was a four-to-six-foot drop into a swirling pool. We were continually pulled into the chaos. We hit the panic stage of exhaustion, frustration, and fearing what would happen next. We were pulled into the current over and over and over again.

In many ways, defining currents, working upstream, downstream, or whichever boat you are in comes back to thinking with your heart and having the courage to take the next first step into what you believe in. Hopefully, the last ten chapters helped define why adventure is a core tenet to designing an adventurous life. It's time to play in the next section!

Key Takeaways

When navigating the waters and currents of normal, consider these key takeaways:

- Embrace the calm. Don't wish away the parts of your life that might seem easy in the moment for more adventure.
- Water can be relaxing and terrifying.
- Recognize we may not be in the same boat, and we may not have the same intentions as others in our life. It's okay.
- There will be times when you want simply float downstream, but often that is the status quo of life.
- Working upstream utilizes energy and resources; it's easier when there is a tribe of people working alongside you headed in the same direction.
- Don't assume someone who is in a different current needs to be saved. The way to learn about someone's life, or the currents of their lifestyle, is by asking questions.
- We connect to those we have relationships with. If you are looking for a tribe, put yourself in proximity to others you admire.

Part 3: Play Wildly

Exactly Enough

"When starting out, don't worry about not having enough money. Limited funds are a blessing not a curse. Nothing encourages creative thinking in quite the same way."
—H. Jackson Brown

If I put my pragmatic glasses on, growth is not linear. We spike and lull at different times of the year and different ages of our life. The forces of the universe want us to think in urgency:

"The back-to-school sale ends Sunday."

"Get it now, or you will miss out."

If you want a nerdy project, pick some products, and study the "sale prices" over an extended period of time. Very few prices are static. They are constantly changing.

Having Enough

Through marketing and the sense of urgency, society plays on our emotions and works hard to instill some FOMO. Another timeline that sends parents, schools, and communities into a tizzy is something like third-grade reading scores. If kids aren't reading at this level by this time, they won't (fill in the narrative).

Do you know there are very few benchmarks in life that actually need to happen within a developmental stage? One of the few is the ability to speak our native language.

Most milestones are based on someone else's definition of enough. A sense of urgency supports the scarcity mindset. I sometimes wonder what would happen if we all simply believed we already had enough. Enough time, enough money, enough power. What if you already had everything you needed in life?

I have met many successful people in life. Many were striving to achieve the next thing. At work, it might be a job title. In sports, it might be the title of world champion. In school, it might be a GPA or class rank—the benchmark for the elusive definition of *enough*. Maybe it's a certain dollar amount, a certain car, or an aspect of your house that aligns with having enough. What is enough?

If we go back to Chapter 6, most often *enough* and *success* have similar themes. We determine which rung on the ladder we have our sights on. "Guilt is the byproduct of striving." Have you ever talked to someone one year after they have reached their dream? After the awe wears off, reality doesn't align with their expectations. They wonder, *This is it?* or *Now what?* It's common after a summit or being named "the best." Many even experience depression. The world keeps moving.

Slicing Your Pie

You can't sit at the top forever; at some point, you must come down. Very few have prepared for the coming-down phase, which is why when I talk to people who are retiring, I ask, "What is your plan for month two?" Everyone has their plans for the first day or week, but many have been working thirty plus years. It takes at least sixty days to form new habits. Creating some intention around what you want day thirty to look like is a piece of a much larger puzzle.

If each day was a pie, how would you slice it? Whom would you share it with? I remember participating in a conflict training one day when the facilitator said, "Don't give away your entire pie right away, or you'll have nothing left over for when you get hungry." It's a strange quote, but it has helped me visualize my energy currency each day.

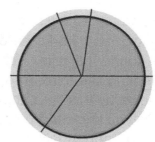

Who or What gets a slice of your life pie?

If the day starts with conflict or worry, something that consumes my energy, then it depletes my tank and doesn't leave much for the things that need my energy later. Most often, I see this with working parents. They give everything to their job and come home to their family depleted.

What if you already have everything you need? What if our kids already had enough? They don't need travel hockey or the gymnastics team that you endure as part-time taxi. My parents sometimes tell me they didn't have enough money for us to do travel sports. From my perspective, I didn't ask to do travel sports. I do believe we have enough.

Success in Fun

I am reminded of the mantra "Every day felt like a vacation." Vacation for many people does not include travel. It's often spending time doing something you love, or experiencing an adventure. What if instead of wishing for a new pie, we just sliced it differently each day? My "Recreation and Fun" slice of my pie is quite large. When I defined indicators of success in that slice, it was revealing:

- How much did I laugh today?
- Did I do something that I genuinely enjoyed doing (not something I have to do)?
- Can I write down one thing I did with each child today that I feel good about?
- How much time did I spend outside?

While these are not indicators in a research sense, they are questions that can guide our data-collection efforts—to establish some baseline numbers—to better understand what success in the recreation and fun slice of the pie looks like in this season of life.

Finding the Trail Markers

As a recovering achiever, it's helped me better understand what I am working toward in life. They are not traditional SMART goals. For me, they are a blend of trail markers as I listen to my inner voice, feeling my way through it.

The slices of the pie that many use to define success often correspond with money and work. I spent so much of my thirties working toward the next rung on the ladder in my career, waiting for the day I'd hit six figures in income.

The interesting thing was when I got to where I thought I wanted to go, I had the month-after-summit experience, where I realized I wasn't sure I wanted to be there.

It's not just an impostor syndrome thing. I felt worthy of being there. I was looking for my money metric to give me permission to do the things I wanted to do in life.

What? It was an interesting discovery. Six figures drifted me into a scarcity mindset, and yet the things we were spending money on were not the things that brought us joy.

I was also influenced by the money story of my family growing up. Throughout my life, my dad worked two or three jobs, seven days a week. He often worked shifts that aligned with our sleeping time. He would go to work after dinner, or on the weekends at 4:00 a.m. to be home by noon. When I asked him why he worked so much, he simply said, "Because I had to."

I thought we needed the money. Working hard and grinding through life seemed like a normal part of our money story. I recall being in the car once when my mom deposited some money into his bank account. I saw the receipt and was surprised at the balance. I had a hard time converting that balance into the years of his life he lost in sleep. What if he traded half of the hours he worked for more sleep? Would he be a happier and healthier human being? We will never know the answer to this question.

The Fallacy of Money

Having enough relates to the value of our expectations. In some weird way, I wanted to get enough money, so I didn't have to worry about working so hard or as many jobs as my dad. "Enough Money" mindset was one of life's fallacies. After some work, my husband and I have come to realize that we are most aligned and joyful on a $70,000 a year budget, so that is what we plan our life around now. Everything else, we automate around savings, investing, and giving. We play with the numbers, and if a season of our life comes where we need to increase the spend or trim back the spend, we know how to do that and put in some checkpoints.

Exactly What You Need

Enough is far more than money. This past summer, I was adamant about spending time with the kids, adventuring, unplugging, and doing just enough to keep things moving forward. Part of that was parent life after fifteen months of COVID, and part was my adventure mom busting out.

I promised myself when the kids were back in school, I'd have time to do all the things I *should* be doing. Guess what happened when September came? I didn't do any of it. I sulked around. All I could think about was our next adventure. Everything felt like work. I avoided the to-do list and felt guilty. Guilty for not being productive enough. When I was given a gift of time, I literally blew it.

One Sunday morning, after my husband and kids headed out hunting at 6 a.m., I was trying to muster up some willpower to tackle my growing to-do list. I looked at it and said out loud, "But I don't want to do any of this!"

Then a thought occurred to me. *Well then, Heidi, what do you* **want** *to do today?*

Creating that list felt lighter. The list changed slightly, but I was excited about a few things that were previously on the to-do list. That change in mindset of "have to" to "want to" shifted the energy. I did several of the items and enjoyed the day.

As I went to bed that night, I thought about that to-do list, and I was reminded, *what if we have everything we need inside of us*? What if the two weeks of unproductive time were exactly what I needed? Why was I so interested in attaching my self-worth to my productivity? I don't have an answer for you. It's a journey I continue to work through.

Enough Time

Time is the one non-renewable resource many seem to be in search of. I have not found the magic wand to make more time, but I have found ways to get intentional about my time. Two strategies that I utilize are *the knowing-doing gap* and *focused and unfocused time strategies.*

A deep dive on the knowing-doing gap is coming in an upcoming chapter, but in a nutshell, it's a way to move beyond our thoughts into action. Neuroscience has demonstrated over that multitasking is the detriment of productivity. Focus time is a way to remove distractions and work on a singular task; however, it needs to be limited as our brains fatigue from the intensity of focus time; therefore, unfocus time is also important.

Focus and Unfocus Time

I like to think of focus time as "thinking tasks." They might include tracking critical details like financial data, writing an essay, or studying research. Unfocus time is more loosely structured and ideal for creativity and problem-solving.

Creating the space for both to exist in your life is important. For me, focus time has always been more challenging. I often relate to the quotation, "My brain is like an internet browser. I have nineteen tabs open, three are frozen, and I have no idea where the music is coming from."

I would describe myself as unstructured and spontaneous as opposed to structured and planned. I would procrastinate and use deadlines to get me to focus on a major project, binging my way to a finish line. Focus time and deadlines like to squeeze out the presence of unfocused time.

Unfocused time was most often when recreation and play were present in my life. When I squeeze those out to hit a deadline, my overall joy, metrics for thriving, and well-being suffered. I needed a couple of hacks to ease the burden of structured and planned focus time. To spread out responsibilities over a long period of time instead of jamming into a tight and unrealistic deadline. These are a few of my tricks for having "enough time."

Create an Information and Idea Funnel

I know my memory isn't as strong when there are so many things swirling in it. My life improved significantly when I learned to do a daily purge. I am a bit of a journal and notebook hoarder. I have thoughts, to-do lists, meal ideas, and adventure notes all over the place. Then I learned a system to funnel them all into one place.

I took a training called Effective Edge by InteraWorks (more information in the resource section), where I learned how to empty my brain into one place. I use it most consistently for work-related items, but the principles apply to so many different areas of my life. Now, when my brain gets swirly, I get the thoughts or ideas into the funnel and assign each a category and a due date.

Getting things into one place, creating the system to sort through and take action has been a game-changer for me. I spent five hours setting up the system during the online training, and then it's ten minutes a day of clearing my brain and getting all that stuff into the funnel.

Whether you use a funnel or not, getting the ideas out of your head allows them to stop taking up brain bandwidth. You can release the responsibility of remembering anything related to that task or idea. That alone was a huge energy boost.

Time Blocking

Notice when you are most *in the zone*. I try to schedule my most thoughtful work during that time. My brain is least busy first thing in the morning and late at night when it's quiet and calm in our house. The bulk of this book was written between the hours of 5:30–6:30 a.m. and 8:00–10:00 p.m. Ironically, my most productive time is 2:30–4:00 p.m. That seems to be my power hour when I can complete a considerable number of tasks.

I aim to do solo adventures over the lunch period if possible. During the week, it's usually a walk, hike, or trip to a park or a lake. My intention is by 5:00 p.m. to be completely unstructured and available to play and connect with kids. These aren't long periods— maybe fifteen to thirty minutes. We try to have family adventure or connection routines during supper and immediately after.

Time blocking works as a general framework for us. Noticing things like when we are most alert, when we need a break, and when we feel a sense of urgency in our natural rhythms is the key. I am often surprised how little time is needed to do things when I remove distractions and commit to doing them.

Removing Distractions

There is power in creating either barriers or incentives to help improve outcomes. Some people need a clean desk to do creative work. I have noticed when I am working on strategic things, I like music in the background. When I am doing a reset or taking a break, I like to go outside and listen to the sounds of nature and feel the elements or take some deep breaths. I take a shower to signal major transition time. Often, it's after work or before bed to give my brain the cue to turn down.

It never failed. I would be working on a big group project and feel stuck. My colleagues started to give me a hard time because every time I left a strategy session, I'd come back from the restroom with an idea. Neuroscience agreed. Stepping away from what you are working on removes distractions.

I set boundaries with technology by turning off all notifications in email, social media, and most of those on my phone. The pinging of the computer or phone rarely rises to the level of an emergency that needs my attention. I have established the simple understanding with those around me that if something is an emergency (and I say emergency because I learned that everyone's definition of urgent is different), then call me. Otherwise, I check messages and emails two or three times a day (morning, midday, and end of day), and I will get back to them then. If someone sounds urgent, I often ask, "When do you need this by?"

One of the *aha* moments was if an email needed action, it would go into the funnel. For some reason, when I think of removing distractions, I am reminded of the scene in the movie *For the Love of the Game.* Kevin Costner is a pitcher and says, "Clear the mechanism," and the entire world around him blurs, and the sounds muffle to the equivalent of white noise. When I am trying to do focus work, I like to use that visual of "clear the mechanism" and blur all the noise around me and create some barriers so others can't get into my space when I am in that zone.

Block Schedule

A way to protect chunks of focus time is through blocking and tackling my schedule. I hear people say they don't have time to do fun things. I have experienced that as well. I was letting my calendar and the to-do list determine what I got to do each day. Then I started blocking out time on my calendar for the things I wanted to do.

I use time blocking for at least two-hour chunks of time. I highly value personal development, and it was never making its way into my life. I began scheduling blocks of time for intentional learning on Wednesday afternoons and protecting that time so others couldn't steal it. It was a commitment I made to keep that time sacred.

When I go through my funnel each week, I schedule a block of time for the items in the funnel so I can make sure they get done, and I remove the distractions. I also know that things come up, so having boundaries and space in my day to respond is important for me.

When family adventure became a priority, we scheduled an adventure at least once a month. The goal for me in these time blocks is not actually about productivity but more about creativity and exploration. Tackling is the productivity aspect of ticking off items and making progress. Be mindful that you need space for both. We were not designed to be robots and productivity machines.

Prep Your Mind and Body

One of our many airport stories started on a summer day in a Dallas, Texas, when my kids were all exhausted. I was being the mom I wanted to be. I know that's an odd statement, given the conditions. How many parents are the best version of themselves at an airport when things seem completely out of our control? How many parents are the best version of themselves when their kids are tearing things up and exhausted in a public place?

I was so prepared for things to be out of my control, for the kids to be exhausted and challenging, that I was ready. It's during these times when our best version is needed; if we take care of ourselves along the way, the outcomes can be much better. Walking into that airport, I knew one of the few things I had control over when traveling was how I showed up and reacted to various things throughout the day. I am at the mercy of the airlines to potentially change gates or have a delayed flight.

I knew my kids were tired, which might mean rational thoughts would be harder to find. I did a five-minute meditation in the car as we approached the airport. I slowed my breathing and mentally stepped into being a calm and patient mom. I would likely need to offer piggybacks or escalator rides to make the day tolerable. Walking into the airport with that mindset and being physically ready for anything helped me be the mom that was needed for that moment, which turned out to be less than stellar.

My eighteen-month-old had a complete temper tantrum because I wouldn't let him play with the bubbler (that is Wisconsin slang for a drinking fountain, I have come to learn) while someone else was waiting for it. He also attempted to run onto a random flight at the Kansas City airport while we were walking by the gate. My daughter decided she couldn't walk. My oldest son's backpack was too heavy. With each dose, I just kept accepting life as it was, moving forward with a compassionate persona. By the way, this is not a natural state for me to be in. It takes a *lot* of energy for me to stay calm, as I tend to be a pretty jacked-up ball of energy.

There are other examples of preparing your mind and body for an experience. I think about sports. I had a routine that I would go through before high jumping. When I get ready to record a podcast, I need to be energized and excited. Some days that comes naturally, and other days, I need to do a little prep work to get there. I might crank up some music and have a spontaneous dance party or do some super yoga pose to ground me into a quiet place.

Getting our body and mind ready for the desired activity is helpful to achieve a positive overall outcome. We do our best when we are in the flow state—when our brains and bodies are in alignment.

A Clear Ending Time

Having worked in complex systems, I know it is easy to go down rabbit holes. While the vision can be exciting, it can also feel overwhelming. I like to set timers to limit my time on a task. I might commit to working on a project for forty-five minutes before taking a hard break so I can get up and walk away from the work. Or I might offer myself an incentive if I commit to doing something I have been dreading.

Breaking those big scary things into simple next steps helps me make progress. I try to end each sprint with the question, "What is the next first step?" so I don't leave myself hanging with possibilities. Creating boundaries and removing distractions helps me stay focused on what I have intended to focus on during the blocks of time I have set.

Productivity Trap

In many ways, we have tied success to how much more we can do with less. I appreciate efficient systems that can make my life easier. I have also questioned, at what cost? Why is the focus always on doing more?

What if we flipped it and decided to do less instead? That is a hard concept to embrace. I really struggled with the idea of doing less, but I also knew doing less meant deeper connections and greater impact. My theme for 2018 was "Be still." I remember how unnerving it was to even think of being still. My normal was high-strung stress offset by high-strung adrenaline.

On the podcast, I invite listeners to join a sixty-day Everyday Adventure Challenge. A previous participant was in the final quarter before a gap year, balancing high stress with high adrenaline, and was planning to decompress at the start of the gap year. I challenged them to practice decompressing right away rather than matching their stress with adrenaline. It takes continuous practice.

Notice what keeps going on the someday/maybe list. Why is it there? Are they the things we don't feel we are good enough to do, so we avoid them? In 2018, I had a hard time sitting to read a book. I had never meditated for more than a few minutes. I could not turn my brain off. I needed a purpose to do anything, and that purpose seemed to be tied to productivity. Regardless of how stressed out I was, I would continue to create a pipe dream to-do list. I asked myself, "If this is my life now, how would I possibly be able to decompress in financial independence?"

We would need to practice slowing down, decompressing, or doing less long before we needed to be good at those things. I think part of the reason people who retire experience depression is related to their purpose and worth being tied to their productivity. If you achieved what you were working toward, what is the next thing? When the career makes way for other opportunities, we assume it's like being on vacation, except we aren't leaving home and we have nothing to do. It might be cool for the first day, but lifestyle changes don't happen in a day. It takes continuous practice over several months to rebuild the brain, body, and emotional self.

Key Takeaways

The abundance mindset is the belief we have enough. These are some of the strategies for having "enough time."

- Create an information and idea funnel. Create a system to get things out of your head and into a system that works for you.
- Time block. Assign times of day that are most conducive for the type of task that needs to be done.
- Remove distractions. Multitasking is a distraction.
- Block schedule. Assign times to work on the items in the information and idea funnel with some unstructured time built in for breaks.
- Prepare your mind and body.
- Have a clear ending time. Use a timer, and limit the amount of time you allow to work on a task.

What if instead of doing more with less, we flipped it to do less with more?

The Ping-Pong Effect

"Comparison is the thief of joy."
—Unknown

I seldom feel a sense of equilibrium in my life. If one area of my life is thriving, it usually means I am drawing energy and time from another area of my life. After some time, I try to equal out the time and balance the energy. Ironically, I go from feeling crazy busy and overscheduled to bored and unstructured. It feels like I am playing a never-ending game of ping-pong by myself.

The functional roles we play in life often land in our laps based on responsibility or choice. For example, if you look at the functional roles I chose to play as a mom, you might see me as the primary adventure planner, empathetic listener, thought leader, menu planner, idea generator, life systems creator, and photographer. I also have the responsibility of being the financial investor, chief home operations officer, sanitation crew, and backpack and homework auditor.

The roles we play in our life are not static. We might even feel roles are forced and unattainable, that we will never be good enough for them.

First and foremost, *you are already good enough*! I once looked for validation and permission externally. What I found was external pressures that caused me to question my worth and compare my low days to someone else's highlight reels. Little good came from it.

Our brains are plastic not static. They are ever-evolving and designed to continue learning from those around us. Our physiology is not designed to be the expert in everything but to solve the problem in front of us. We already have the answers to most of life's questions; we just need to believe our answer is correct, or even better, be okay moving forward with it being wrong. We need a different type of learning experience.

Land of a Thousand Ladders

Let me bring you to the land of a thousand ladders. Imagine you are in a gorgeous ravine. There are ladders all around you leading out. However, the rungs on the ladder only appear when you learn something from someone else. Each ladder represents a different aspect of life you are working to improve. The only way to get out is to learn your way to the next rung. There are a thousand ladders because there is more than one way out of the ravine; you don't even have to get out because at the bottom of the ravine is a refreshing pool. At any time, you can make a lateral move to another ladder. People are above and below you on the ladders.

> Life is a land of a thousand ladders.
> There is always more than one way up.
> There are always others ahead of you on the journey.
> You will also be ahead of others on their journey.

Who's Ahead of You

In life, we often only see the person at the top of the ladder. But they are so far up the ladder; it is hard for them to help you. Between you and the person at the top of the ladder, there might be ten other people who have been where you are currently. The individuals who are the next rung or two ahead of you also have experience. They have struggled and succeeded. They may have moved to a different ladder to get where they are now.

Notice who is ahead of you on the ladder—not just the person at the top of the ladder, but also who is two or three rungs up. Are they willing to turn around from time to time and reach a hand back to help others up? Or are they afraid that those behind might pass them up, so they push them down to try to keep them in their place? Observe who is ahead of you on these ladders. Those individuals might be who you want to accept advice from. We love to glorify and expect to reach the top of the ladder quickly. When we compare ourselves to others, we make many unvalidated assumptions about them.

I think one of the reasons I find myself in ping-pong mode is burnout. I lose energy and momentum. I move on to something else or lack consistency causing me to stop reaching for the next rung. I have also noticed I don't always ask for help from the people ahead of me.

Usually, when I am in a lull, I find the greatest push comes from those behind me. When I reach out to help others, it gives me a boost. It's like their energy and curiosity are the push I need to get to that next rung as well. How are you reaching back to help others on the ladder behind you?

Switching Ladders

At any time, you can move to a different ladder and learn different things. In fact, you already do about thirty-five times a day with each decision and role change you make. I use the land of ladders as a metaphor because we learned subjects in school as a linear progression, and the goal was to reach the top, or I guess in the world of standardized tests, *exceed expectations*. To get to point B, you had to first stop at point A.

With a thousand different ladders, you don't have only one pathway to keep climbing. We can climb as high as we wish on the ladder. Learning is more than the head work of "knowing." The next rung is attained by taking action. From my experience, learning seldom happens alone. Even if we prefer to work alone, our learning path is influence by community, with people inspiring, challenging, and supporting us up the ladder.

The Roles We Choose

We noticed parents ahead of as taxi drivers, scurrying kids to and from many different activities. I was aware of this role and figured it was inevitable at some point. But then I questioned, "What if I don't want taxi driver to be a key role?"

We can choose a different path, a different ladder. None of the roles are required rites of passage. Here are some of the ways we avoided the taxi driver role:

- Limiting choices for our children to participate in extra activities (They may choose one activity per season.)
- Using the divide and conquer method where my husband and I split up to take on responsibility for different kids and rotate if possible
- Outsourcing to others who could carry some of the roles such as taxi driver or support squad.

I avoided the soccer mom role for a considerable amount of time. The rungs on the ladders don't need to be defined by outcomes, either. The idea of the taxi driver role felt really depleting. The story I was telling myself about that role was based on external comparison and pressures of what I thought I needed to be.

One day, I saw a few other moms using practice time to do solo adventures, read a book, or have connection time with the remaining family members. By learning from those on the next rung up, I was able to reframe my expectations of the role of soccer mom by asking, "How might we have a joy-filled family life without having to be a taxi driver?"

Transition as Reflection

After each season of activity, we saw major transition periods. That offered great reflection times to pull out the Joy Audit. After each child finished a season, we discussed their Joy Rating—was it worth it? After a few years of playing little league, my daughter shared that she would rather be playing on the playground than on the baseball field. While she enjoyed the game, there were other things she'd rather do. The next baseball season, she took cooking classes.

There will always be ladders or roles in life where we have more experience than others. In designing a life of adventure and embracing the sherpa philosophy, we also have a responsibility to bring others up the ladder with us. We might never be the expert in all the things. We are constantly learning, dreaming, and growing. As the world evolves, so do the possibilities of who we can become.

The Podcasting Ladder

The development of *Ordinary Sherpa* was based on finding and building a community of people in the realm of adventure. When I embarked on this journey as an adventurous working mom, there were few role models and mentors I found. Ten years later, as we considered traveling the world with kids, we wanted to connect with other families who shared our love for adventure and could potentially meet up so our kids could connect with other kids when we traveled.

I started the podcast to have conversations with other families who were ahead of us. We might not have considered the ladder they were climbing prior to having the conversation. The Sherpa philosophy of being a few steps ahead of others really resonated. I am rarely the expert, and there will always be others ahead of me, but if I can offer support and help connect to others ahead of me, then that is a win-win.

If I reach out to someone, and they try to keep me in my place, it's time to find a new ladder and work around them. They aren't my people, and I don't need their permission to get to the next rung on the ladder. I look for people willing to reach back from time to time. Those are also the people I also want to give a boost from below and help them rise to the next level. Even ladders have a push-and-pull effect.

When trying to find your tribe, I suggest you look for three to four people who are a few rungs ahead of you on the ladders you want to climb. Give generously to help push them forward. Get curious. Are they offering a hand back? I look for the helpers!

Seismic Shifts

I want to be aware of and anticipate these large shifts in time and energy. I recall in the spring of 2021 (in the United States), as vaccines became available and the world was beginning to open up, people were so eager to see and do things again; they began filling their calendars with travel, hobbies, and social gatherings. I could see the ping-pong ball ready to accompany a seismic shift of energy in the opposite direction, only to once again be overwhelmed with busyness. I knew it was coming, and I still ended up on the ping-pong table.

I tend to thrust myself (and our family) into the opposite action. If life is calm and still, we tend to throw ourselves into lots of activity. If we are overscheduled and burned out, we tend to seek an escape, quiet time. We veg out and decompress. The challenge with the ping-pong lifestyle is always running away from what we currently have. I can't tell you how many people I talk to who simply use vacations as an escape or call self-care "spa days." I think, in the end, the goal is to design a life you aren't running away from.

When you accept that you have the right to choose the path that is best for you and decide which ladders you are interested in climbing, you can feel free to lounge in the ravine a little longer. When we finally stand in the place and claim, "This is what I want my life to be" without seeking permission from everyone else around us, that is the day we have finally made it!

Key Takeaways

Only you can determine which ladders to climb and what you want your life to look like.

- Find three or four people who are a few rungs ahead of you on the ladders you want to climb. Give generously to help push them forward and get curious. Are they offering a hand back? Look for the helpers.
- Who's a few rungs behind you? Are they pushing you forward and helping you up? Are you reaching back to help them? We refer to this as the Sherpa philosophy of community building.
- When you continue to run away from the life you have and maintain the ping-pong effect, you keep the balls in the air and hold up the system. The goal is to design a life you don't need to run away from.

Knowing, Doing, Being

"A lot of people in our industry haven't had very diverse experiences. So, they end up with very linear solutions without a broad perspective on the problem. The broader one's understanding of the human experience, the better design we will have."
—Steve Jobs

By far, the hardest thing I've ever had to do is actually do the work. Coming up with ideas or different ways to solve a problem has never been a challenge for me. The excitement would usually fuel me, and I'd throw myself into learning how to make it all work. But the moment it was time to do the work, the speed of my progress slowed to a crawl. In some ways, less knowing leads to greater doing. The expectation that we need to know what we are doing suddenly creates a barrier to overcome.

Collecting Gurus

When I bought a course to learn how to podcast, I was excited and expected I would learn what equipment to buy, how to hit record, sound good, and hit publish. When the course revealed things like brand development, finding my voice, my host persona, creating a website, building an email list, claiming my social handles, etc., as the beginner steps, I wasn't sure if I was up for the challenge.

Each step can be so big, and I just didn't know how to do it. I like to say, "No one really knows until they do." I was buying courses and reading books from gurus. I like to refer to the stage of hoarding knowledge as collecting gurus. I didn't really know how to podcast until I had an audience. You don't get an audience by studying the craft. You have to actually do the work. Doing the work is the daily action that creates progress.

Knowledge Vomit

There are plenty of armchair experts who might hear about your experiences and tell you what they know. I like to check in with my energy bank account during moments like these. Is this knowledge dump going to add or deplete my energy? As Brené Brown would say, "If you aren't in the arena getting your ass kicked on occasion, I'm not interested in your feedback. There are a million cheap seats in the world today filled with people who will never be brave with their own lives but will spend every ounce of energy they have hurling advice and judgment at those of us trying to dare greatly."

As a receiver of this knowledge vomit, I sometimes need to remind myself that this spewing knowledge on us can come from a place of care and love. They might want to connect with us, and sharing knowledge is one way they might think they are helping us. I haven't personally found knowledge disguised as advice helpful, which is why I also refrain from being the knowledge giver.

If someone is curious about my thoughts, knowledge, or experience, it starts with them asking me questions. Likewise, if I am trying to get others on board with my idea, I begin by asking them questions and getting curious about their thoughts, ideas, and perceptions. This is a skill I am building. I realized sharing my enthusiasm without others asking questions looks like I am trying to sell my closest friends and family members on my ideas. We can invite them to the conversation and codesign potential experiences if there is interest.

Adventure Advisor Circle

A critical element that led to substantial growth in our adventure family lifestyle was the people we included in our tribe—those who added to our energy bank accounts. Our adventure advisor circle is comparable to our trusted advisor circle—the experts we trust with our most valuable assets. In our trusted advisor circle, we are willing to be vulnerable with financial, health, legal, career, and family insider knowledge.

People who inspire us can be critically honest and uplifting. They are who we trust and have built a relationship with over time. We may have curated our advisor circle after years of feeling depleted by others who felt the need to dump knowledge, worry, and doubt. Our adventure tribe is different from our typical friends and family circle, although I do have several that overlap. Given our choice to pursue a beyond-normal lifestyle, it's not something most of our traditional friends and family circles have experience or interest in.

My adventure advisor circle includes individuals from all different walks of life who have specific expertise that I find value in. When I connect with them, they add to my energy account. Our adventure tribe includes people who have lived a different lifestyle. Some might have a different approach to earning money; some have experience in credit card travel rewards. We are inspired by how others approach educating their kids and value personal development. Still others have lived a more traditional life but are enthusiastically supportive of each risk we take beyond normal. I don't have a magic formula for who belongs in the tribe or how many to include; I just knew I needed a tribe.

To Whom We Listen

It has taken me a while to distinguish the tribe members as a critical element to overall lifestyle design. One of the first qualifiers of whom I receive knowledge from are people who have experience with the ladder I want to climb. For example, I was once talking about taking a trip to Mexico, and someone decided they should tell me how dangerous it is—the cartels are running in the streets, killing people in broad daylight. My first question was, "Really? Have you been there?" Their response told me how to rank that information.

If I am curious, I keep asking questions to learn more. I give more weight and curiosity to those with experiences I am looking to create. The people I learn from and listen to will have a big impact on my progress.

One of the main reasons I created a community is because finding people with the experiences I want to create are out there but can be hard to find. Rather than following someone's content, I wanted to create human connections with those craving adventure experiences. I wanted more than knowledge and content. I wanted to interact with others who have similar goals and experiences.

131

If I had listened to all the people who thought I needed to stop traveling/camping/skiing/(fill in the blank) when we had children, I would never be where I am today.

If we put all the weight in knowledge in our pack, it's pretty heavy and much harder to lift. Being selective and choosing what to pack in the doing phase is critical. My theory is to pack light and fail fast. I try to move quickly with a little bit of information and prefer action testing overconsuming content.

Making Doing Easier

Oversaturating ourselves with knowing doesn't make doing any easier. We can only learn so many things before we simply hunker down and do it. The only way to build that website was to sit down with the video tutorials and do the next thing. One reasons I included Perceptions of Success and the Wheel of Life in the early chapters is because it is easy to distinguish what the next step will be with technical procedures and logical patterns.

When your action step is to spend time one-on-one with your child or suggest to your partner a dream to take a gap year, there isn't exactly a guide to walk you through what to expect next. To make progress, we must be willing to explore bravely. The response might send us back into knowing before taking action. It might even be a repeat of the first action attempt that failed.

When we first considered the idea of living life differently, it was heavily focused on extensive travel. I began binging content on travel rewards. I followed all the technical steps using credit card sign-up bonuses and studying what our strategy would be, and I continued to accumulate various rewards currency to advance our goals. That first redemption was so hard to push the button on. Until then, I had been following the technical guidance of others, but making the decision on what to do with the rewards was a step only I could feel my way through.

There was considerable time and energy spent researching (yes again, collecting gurus), making sure I was optimizing the rewards for the greatest redemption value. I had to experience the emotional, intellectual, and financial efforts that went into the investment.

When I do travel rewards strategy consulting with families, I hear over and over how hard that first redemption is. It gets better with practice. Each time we do the thing, it gets a little easier, and we aren't as emotionally tied to the rewards we had carefully earned through a thoughtful strategy.

Reframe Expectations

Even though travel rewards were part of our overall financial strategy, they lose their value with time, so I had to think of them differently than a traditional investment. Travel rewards needed to be redeemed to provide value. The longer I held them, the less value they would potentially give in the future, either through expiration dates or with companies changing their redemption structures. Travel companies rarely make it easier or require fewer rewards to redeem; the formula almost always goes up. Rather than waiting for the perfect moment to hit Redeem, I remind myself the rewards help us save our income for other things.

Rewards are a tool to help us travel. I needed to decouple the rewards as a way to optimize our investments. I reframed redemptions to focus on the travel experience it would offer. By removing all the other expectations I had tied to a redemption, I am able to underthink my way through the process and redeem the rewards in alignment with my purpose.

Testing the Gap

The space between knowing and doing has been coined the knowing–doing gap. If we take it one step further, the difference between doing and being has a similar gap. I can't just say, "This is in my purpose in life," do it tomorrow, and be there. The only way we get to be the person we want to become and live the life we want to live is to practice it over and over again. Each day, we must take the next first step.

The gap between knowing and doing can be really hard, especially when we are talking about adventurous lifestyle choices or things that might not fall in the sphere of normal. Instead of plan, plan, plan, act, we have to act quickly with few resources at risk. We test little sections of life, work, and play in the chosen experience and ask ourselves, "Does this fit us?" No one can answer that question but those currently living and experiencing it.

The only way to know if something is going to work for you is to do it. Not all experiences are planned. The first time we rented an RV was out of necessity. It was June 2020, and we had just canceled our three-week Hawaii vacation. I was determined to find a way to be completely self-sustained, have little interaction with others, and still have an adventurous vacation experience. The RV was the best way to do that, driving, sleeping, eating, and bathing all under one roof. I had zero expectations, zero experience, and very little planning apart from my years of tent camping and considerable travel with kids.

I never anticipated that less than one year later, we would buy a Class A RV and consider life on the road as a major chapter in our adventure story. The surprise in renting that RV was that it fit us. We didn't even know we wanted it; we were just desperate to get out and experience the world. I didn't believe it at first. We rented another camper later that summer and realized it offered something magic to our family. The following summer, we attempted two weeks while I worked remote full-time only to realize that was not the desired experience.

Perspective Building

By testing and experimenting, I gained perspective of what was reasonable and desirable. Doing it not only provides progress, but it also breathes confidence and clarity into our knowing. What I had been planning came to life in unpredictable ways.

Imagine you want to live on a sailboat but have never sailed before. We might look at a way to create a minimum viable experience—to add a dot to our path. We might sign up for sailing lessons or ask a friend who competes in the regatta if we can volunteer for an upcoming race. There are ways to gain experience without buying a sailboat.

When I design experiences, adding dots to my journey, I think about proximity to others farther along. How can I get close to others who have more experience and learn by being around them, seeing, feeling, and doing as much as possible? I might also look for low-risk entry points that include doing an activity. I would favor sailing lessons that include the opportunity to be a deckhand versus all lessons being knowledge based.

If the solution I am working toward is hiking the Continental Divide Trail, I might start with hiking a certain distance, altitude, or with limited items to mimic the experience. Each of those experiences also informs what we can do better. The more we practice doing, the better the solution will become. Being comes from a series of doing. Being is much easier when we have a tribe of people pushing us up the ladder not pulling us down.

Design Experiences

I have always found this Steve Jobs quotation helpful. "A lot of people in our industry haven't had very diverse experiences. So, they end up with very linear solutions without a broad perspective on the problem. The broader one's understanding of the human experience, the better design we will have." It's a healthy reminder that each dot is an experience, an action; it's doing something. Progress toward being happens over a series of experiences. You can't exactly jump the line from knowing to being; you have to do the thing!

Beyond normal can be a lonely place, having a tribe of people who "get it" or have experience being different from their group of friends. Most of my family do not have the same dots, nor do they have the same vision for my future, so why wouldn't they think I am weird (I prefer "beyond normal" over "weird")? When I embraced this quotation from the perspective of empathy, I stopped feeling like it was my job to get others to buy into my vision.

They didn't have enough experiences to see the potential of my vision. If I wanted to find others who could support and relate to my vision, I needed to create a network of those who had similar dots or had a similar vision. If they didn't have either, I debated whether they belonged in my adventure tribe.

It's not an inclusive or exclusive thing. I could still be friends with them, but I wouldn't weigh their experiences or insights as heavily on my vision. I also wouldn't go to them seeking support for my future vision, as they weren't equipped with the experiences to understand.

Generosity and Receivership

Remember the land of a thousand ladders. Being that source of inspiration to others is also an extremely worthwhile and gratifying experience. I get as much energy from sharing and helping others as I do receiving from others and achieving progress. To maintain that flow of energy, I have boundaries of how much I am willing to invest in others. It is often based on what progress they are making and how they are valuing my time.

I share a considerable amount of content for free, welcome questions, and will engage back and forth for a while with audience members. Action breeds confidence, and while growth and change are never easy, there is a noticeable difference between those who continue to do the thing and those who continue overthinking and wish their way forward.

I am much more willing to invest time in someone who believes in possibility and does the work to make progress. The balance between generosity and receivership is closely linked, and we all know of relationships where the energy balance is leaning in one direction. One of the ways I like to jump the line is to invest in someone who is ahead of me and do so enough to be noticed and appreciated.

When I bought a podcast course from one of my favorite podcasters, I wanted to do all the VIP things to get as much access to him as possible. I also wanted to show that I was worthy of his investment by producing a podcast that made the course stand out. Progress builds not only confidence but also credibility and accountability. There are no wrong answers in moving forward except inaction and continuing to siphon energy from others without ever contributing back.

Consistent Practice

Being is a much longer process than doing. Being means I need to consistently show up and practice the future version of who I want to become. Being isn't a box you can simply check. If I want to be adventurous, I can't sit back in the easy chair and watch Netflix. I can't be a podcaster by simply listening to other podcasts. I can't hike the Continental Divide thru-hike by following other hikers on Instagram. I can't live a van life by subscribing to various YouTube channels. I need to consistently make progress, show up, and add dots to the path toward being that future vision, adjust, and repeat. Knowing and doing are the short-term, quick dots; Doing and being are the long-term, adjust-and-repeat dots.

Key Takeaways

Knowing, doing, and being are not linear steps in a process.
- Knowing is the information we learn. Subscribing to content does not advance your lifestyle goals.
- Doing is taking action on the things we learn. Progress builds confidence, clarity, and credibility.
- Being is consistent action over time to improve your state. Being is long-term thinking.
- Craft your adventure advisor circle with those you trust and have shared vision for your future.
- Determine whom to receive knowledge from on your adventure lifestyle.

Easy Life

"Easy decisions, hard life. Hard decisions, easy life."
—Tim Ferris

We had a saying in our house that came out when we got stuck. "We can do hard things." The funny thing is that 90% of the time, the thing we need to do isn't hard. We have made it hard because we have piled task upon task into the overthinking category. Or we're afraid it's going to be hard, so we avoid it for as long as possible, and now it's staring us in the face. It might even be that we are afraid of what is on the other side.

Simplifying the Overwhelm

Doing builds confidence, and our goal is to do something to keep moving our vision forward. It can be hard to detach from reality long enough to stop thinking and just start doing. Many times, our next step is staring us in the face, and we can't see it because we are focused on the directions two miles ahead.

Instead of submitting to the overwhelm and trying to power through with an inspiring mantra, like, "We can do hard things," I now ask questions like these:

- What's making it hard?
- Does it need to be hard?
- Have I asked for help? Who might be helpful?
- Do I believe in it, or does it feel like a "have to"?
- Do I even have to do it?

It's crazy how quickly we can dissipate overwhelm with simplicity. Often adventure gets clumped into the category of being a "hard thing." If we peel back the onion of adventure, it doesn't have to be hard.

Breaking adventures down into the next first step is much easier to swallow than figuring out how to conquer the entire adventure. For example, what if going camping was reduced to sleeping outside, if hiking a thru-hike was simplified to hiking with a backpack, or deep-sea diving was merely jumping into deep water? Each adventure opportunity has a range of complexity involved.

Treat the adventure like a ladder, with each rung being the next step. If we focus on those adventures with less complexity, less gear, and fewer things that could go wrong, we still build the adventure muscle without as much risk. There will be crossroads where a decision is required. Experience in action-taking builds confidence and enhances progress, making hard decisions less fearful.

Flipping the Script

It's easy to get stuck in a cycle of inaction based on fear of hard decisions. A strategy that gets me unstuck is to simply flip the script. We fear the unknown more than we do the known. While we were working toward our extensive travel plans, I finally flipped the unknown to the known.

What if the life we are living right now is the worst-case scenario? We have an extremely comfortable life that we worked hard for, and it seems everything is in place. My husband and I have good jobs, a comfortable income, a great house in the country, and the kids are doing well academically and socially. But what if we avoid doing extensive travel because of this comfortable life, yet our best life is out there?

My husband and I had so many conversations about the kids missing their friends. I met my best friend when I was eighteen years old, and almost twenty-five years later, we are still friends. I wasn't supposed to meet my friend. I had a different plan to attend a different college but made a last-minute decision to apply to and attend a different school. If we flipped the script from our kids missing their current friends to depriving them of meeting their future best friend, it would change the narrative.

We had conversations about our health and what if we got sick or injured while traveling? Again, we flipped the script. What if we got injured or sick in the next few years and couldn't travel ever again? There are viable and high-quality health care services all over the world. What makes us think our corner of the universe is the only place that could actually treat us?

I think my favorite discussion as of late was "What if we run out of money?" My husband and I have worked continuously since we were fourteen years old—sometimes working two or three jobs at a time. We are pretty gritty and creative people; I'm sure we can get a job or figure something out. The funny thing is, I have known several people now who have left their jobs or retired and simply mentioned to others in their networks if they come across a project they'd like help with, to send them a message. They still had plenty of work at their disposal months later.

Cost of Inaction

When we look at the cost of inaction, we see a period of our kids' lives closing. The opportunity cost of in action in our case will be years of regret. We see our kids' lives getting harder to untangle for extended periods. We see the penalty for staying comfortable and making easy small decisions over and over again.

I can't stress how important it is to begin connecting and reaching out to others to build your adventure tribe and circle of trusted advisors. You can hack the traditional networking strategies and become a superfan. Consume their content, listen to episodes they guest on, or invest in becoming a VIP to skip the line and tap into their brain. Find out as much as you can about the people who have experience tackling the items on your fear list. Don't wait until you are doing the thing to ask the questions or begin consuming content; it's something you can do today.

Creating Your Plan

We know that social capital is something we value. In crafting our adventure plan, we focused on names and faces we had a connection with. We asked each of the kids, "If you could go visit anyone this weekend that you haven't seen in at least six months, whom would you choose to hang out with?" Another question we asked was, "What places have you heard about or seen pictures of that you would like to learn more about or visit someday?" Those questions helped inform our trusted adventure circle to help guide our planning process. We didn't need to plan the entire route. We just needed to have a few key places and people we wanted to visit. We could figure out most of the logistics later.

Listening to other adventure experiences in our advisor circle helped us decide what to do along the way. We had some serious backpackers, a family of mountain bikers, a travel rewards guru, a few RV families, and a minimalist family. Each person in our circle had experience and skills. We didn't need to have all the logistics figured out because we had the expertise and a circle of experienced advisors to ask if we had questions.

The 80/20 Rule

There comes a time when the weight of daily decisions can be heavy. Many small decisions have little impact on the overall trajectory of our life. The small decisions are completely arbitrary and add seemingly little value. If I could bottle up the amount of time I spent deciding what to eat, wear, or do today, just imagine the amount of time and energy I could redistribute to the hard decisions in life. Those easy and relatively meaningless decisions lead to a hard life overall. If you are familiar with The Pareto Principle (the 80/20 rule), you might assume that essentially 20% of people do 80% of the work. I learned a different take on it from Grant Sabatier of *Millennial Money* when he shared a podcast episode highlighting this principle, which became a game-changer in how I approach decision-making.

"The simple idea is that 80% of the results in most areas of your life are actually generated by 20% of your decisions." The reason this became such a mind-blowing discovery was that I didn't need to think or worry about the 80% of decisions I was making every day. I could use my minimalist lens and simplify it down to the hard decisions that really matter and continue to make progress toward our overall life strategy.

The process I used for determining the 20% was heading back to the Wheel of Life and reviewing my metrics for thriving. If the recreation slice of my life was thriving, many other areas of my life seemed to be doing well. By focusing my 20% on thriving in recreation, led to 80% of the other dimensions to be on track.

Long-Term Thinking

The lifestyle we were designing included extensive travel, and I would often daydream about getting there. Escaping life today to a world of travel tomorrow doesn't make all the hard decisions go away. They still find their way into your pack, and you still have to deal with them at some point. Trying to run away from something, hoping to arrive at the happiness stop sounds nice now, but it is not a long-term solution for making hard decisions.

Regardless of where we are in life, we have to make the hard decisions for what we want our life to be. If we don't tackle them or take the time to do the internal work, they will follow us wherever we go. Acknowledging your fears and making progress on the hard decisions is like a little hinge on a big door. It will open doors wider than we imagine.

Key Takeaways

Focusing on the 20% of the hard decisions is a little hinge on a big door.

- What's making it hard?
- Does it need to be hard?
- Have I asked for help? Who might be helpful?
- Do I believe in it, or does it feel like a "have to"?
- Do I even have to do it?

When you get stuck, try flipping the script:

- What if the life we are living right now is the worst-case scenario?
- What if the kids meet their best friend out there, not here?
- What if we got injured or sick in the next few years and can't travel ever again?

What to Do

"Inaction breeds doubt and fear. Action breeds confidence and courage. If you want to conquer fear, do not sit home and think about it. Go out and get busy."
—Dale Carnegie

My default answer to "What should I do?" is, "*Go play!*" I don't care if you are two, twenty-two, forty-two, or eighty-two. Play is a critical element to living a joyful life. Let go of everything on the to-do list and just be four for a while. Leave the expectations and do something right now without any prep. Just be a goofball. Shake off all the expectations. Laugh. Yes, reality will still be there, but give yourself the freedom to stop thinking and just play.

Sourcing Creativity

I like to tap into my creative brain during moments of play and see what I come up with. If you think you are not creative or struggle to come up with ideas, I have two suggestions. First, go back to the section on limiting beliefs (I'm not adventurous chapter) and replace "adventurous" with "creative.' We have everything we need inside us; we just need to draw it out. If that isn't a high priority on your Wheel of Life and metrics for thriving and you'd rather outsource it, then add some creatives to your adventure advisor circle who can inspire you with simple ways to play.

If you'd rather hack my strategy, here is a framework to create many different adventure experiences.

1. Let's start with the happy list—a simple list of thirty things that make you happy or a happy list for each person in the family. Start there as your foundation.
2. I like to think of the process like photo editing. To make a new design, we add layers and filters, resulting in a new

and different experience. I use previous experiences from my happy list as the base photo. Then layer on some of the simple items on my happy list like filters—to use the same image but add different filters for a fun and different look.

3. Let's walk through some examples that help when we are stuck. I use the acronym MAGIC to help me think through how to design new and different experiences.

4. MAGIC is a strategic way to consider and plan for simple adventures that allow us to Play Wildly. Each letter in magic is like a filter on the photo; simply add a filter to an existing item on the happy list item to start. As you build the library of experiences, you can veer away from the happy list if you choose. It's just helpful to start somewhere. This is what MAGIC stands for:

Mismatched
Appearance
Generosity
Impossible
Categories

These help us get unstuck and provide a simple filter to create a new adventure experience.

Mismatched

Psychology research behind mismatch has proven that having an unexpected disruption stimulates different memories and lodges them into long-term memory. A mismatched experience helps dissociate an experience from the trigger that stimulates negative stress, anxiety, or fear. Mismatch adventures are experiences where we might change the order, location, or use different tools. It is an experience where things did not play out as expected. These are some questions we ask when coming up with mismatched adventures, along with some ideas to try:

How might we create mismatched meals?

- Drink milk in wine glasses.
- Pair unlikely foods.
- Eat dinner with chopsticks.

How might we experience our day in reverse?

- Begin the morning with a fun activity usually reserved for the evening. We applied this principle to birthdays and began the day with a big celebration, complete with cake, to start the day.
- Eat dessert for breakfast.

How might we change the location of a typical activity?

- Sleep on the floor.
- Watch a movie in the garage.

How might we use different tools to complete a task?

- Eat with new sand toys instead of dishes and silverware.
- Wrap a gift with toilet paper.
- Use a different form of transportation than you would typically use.

How might we switch roles for who is responsible for what?

- Kids make dinner.
- Parents play video games.

The intent with a mismatch experience is to rewire the brain. By combining two traditionally comfortable things and exposing individuals to a different process and procedure, you can create a unique experience.

Mismatch experiences are not epic adventures. They are usually just weird. Weird is a good way to get out of the comfort zone, and mismatch is a low-risk way to combine two unlikely ideas in a new and interesting experience.

Appearance.

This is thinking through what you want the experience to look like. Often, when we get into planning mode, we start with the tangible things: What are we going to do? When? For this exercise, I want you to put your thinking brain down for a bit and lead with, "How do you want to feel?" If we start from a place of empathy, we can begin to shape the experience on a deeper level. How might we want a person in our group to feel, see, hear, or smell during the experience?

Let me give you an example. I like to do special things for my kids' birthdays, making the experience fun and playful while still very practical. My five-year-old son's travel goal to visit the best ice cream shop in all fifty states. He has a sweet tooth unlike anything I have ever seen! When he asked for pancakes for his birthday dinner, I imagined walking into an ice cream shop. I wanted it to feel like we were at Cold Stone Creamery.

We immediately went through the cupboards and pulled out sauces, flavors, mix-ins, and toppings. It cost virtually nothing. By using empathy and feeling our way through the experience, we were able to transform pancakes for dinner within minutes, having a fun and playful experience similar to a customized ice cream sundae. I wrote down a few recipes for fun pancake ideas:

> Butter Pecan: Mix vanilla syrup (coffee syrup and maple syrup into the pancake batter with crushed pecans. Top with melted butter.
>
> Cookies and Cream: Mix Oreo crumbs into the batter. Top with whipped cream and Hershey's chocolate syrup.
>
> S'mores: Mix graham cracker crumbs into the batter. Top with melted marshmallows and chocolate chips.
>
> Smorgasboard: One mix-in, one sauce, and one topping.

My son and I walked around with the menu and clipboard, taking everyone's order. Each person added their own personal touch with the toppings. As you might guess, the whipped cream got out of hand, making the experience even more memorable. The kids, parents, and grandparents had so much fun *pretending we were little kids in an ice cream shop.* The appearance of the experience was designed from that feeling we wanted of being a kid in an ice cream store.

Engaging Others in Planning

When we plan our travel adventures, I usually start by working through how we want to feel. After a day of travel, we are restless, we feel cooped up, and usually, all our traditional systems are simply off from functioning on someone else's schedule. Our day-after-travel day (for ease of this example, we'll call this day two) is usually a pretty big adventure. That is partly because everyone needs to burn some energy, and they have been carrying around the excitement. It's often something that doesn't require a large investment or structure because it's also a day we simply need to let loose. Day three, however, is a mild, more chill day and a day of acclimation where we might connect with locals or sleep in if we choose. Knowing our rhythms and how we want to feel during the experience helps me visualize how the experience should appear. Here is an easy way to get input and help design how an experience appears.

Ask each family member, "What do you picture when I share these words?"

Cozy	Chill or relaxed
Thrill-seeking	Dread
Scary	Skeptical
Joy	Fun

I also might follow up with what they think might be possible with an experience. For example, when we were planning to be in Hawaii for three weeks, I asked all the kids to share what they thought Hawaii would be like. "What do you think we could do?" Gathering specific yet simple feedback is extremely helpful in guiding the next phase of designing the experience.

Generosity

Generous adventures can be experiences where we contribute our time, talents, or money to help someone else without expecting anything in return. Science has shown that individuals who volunteer live longer, happier lives. A Harvard study found when people performed kind acts every day for seven days, they felt better about themselves. In addition, another Harvard study showed that older adults who volunteered for as little as two hours a week improved their overall sense of well-being compared to those who didn't volunteer. Contributing makes us feel better. It doesn't matter what we contribute or how much. The simple act of giving something to help others improves our overall well-being.

Some generous adventures we can practice in our everyday life or in our own backyard include doing a roadside clean-up, being neighborly by waving, or simply showing random acts of kindness. Last year, we made "Boo Bags" as a way to reverse trick-or-treating (similar to May Day Baskets). We have also celebrated birthdays by donating to a cause that could benefit more than our kids with more stuff. How can we teach our family to be good stewards of the land by practicing leave-no-trace principles? Sometimes it's not an "extra" thing but simply modeling kindness to the earth and appreciating the gifts we have to take care of.

Generosity while adventuring can also look like using our talents to show appreciation. One example is my kids making pictures and writing thank-you notes to flight attendants, which led to us meeting the pilots and having a much richer travel experience.

How can we approach an adventure experience from a place of gratitude and generosity? How can we make someone's day a little better? When we traveled to Hawaii in June of 2021, we knew Hawaii tourism was hit hard with COVID, and we approached all the small businesses with a lens of curiosity and gratitude. During a conversation with a coffee shop owner, we learned more about the coffee beans he harvests in the local community where he grew up and how his uncle (who came to visit while we were there) survived one of the worst tsunamis the United States has ever experienced. Approaching an experience from generosity led to a deeper connection with locals, learning about the history and a location that we likely wouldn't experience without that connection.

Receivership

Adventures might also include receiving someone else's generosity. My brother was a drummer throughout most of his teens and twenties. This year, my son added "drummer" to his identity and was eager to embrace a new skill. My brother wanted to contribute to my son's adventure and offered his drum set since he wasn't using it. Accepting that gift was hard at first. However, it has led to a much greater connection between my son and my brother. It had also allowed my brother to share his talents in a way that he couldn't when the drums were sitting in the attic of his house.

While this might not seem "adventurous," the act of receivership is one that needs practice for some individuals. The story continues when we walked down the streets of Hollywood and a street drummer invited my son to play with him. He was able to say yes. Drumming on five-gallon buckets with a street performer and a crowd forming was an experience that not everyone is able to receive. We rounded out that experience with a generous donation in the street drummer's tip jar.

There have been numerous times while traveling when things didn't go according to plan—such as the story I told earlier about the time my three-year-old daughter got sick and continued to vomit all morning all through the airport and onto the plane. The generosity and kindness we received from so many families have forever seared a space of gratitude in our adventuring hearts. I will never forget the strangers and workers who insisted my focus be on my daughter and her well-being and not on cleaning up a mess.

Generous adventures have become our favorites, in part because it's often an unexpected experience: teaching kindness. Our experiences mimic the results of that Harvard studies—we genuinely feel better when we share our gifts with others.

Impossible

What feels like an impossible adventure? I instantly think of climbing Mount Everest, which is part of the reason I chose the Sherpa tribe as inspiration. Also, *Sherpa* means being willing to guide others through uncharted territory. What is something that seems impossible that you want to work toward? How can you begin to take the next first step?

I will never forget being a camp counselor and hearing campers' ideas of impossible things—things like deep-sea diving, food fights, and swimming across the lake. As staff, we started with the next first step.

For deep-sea diving, we took rowboats to the middle of the lake. Each camper was bundled in a life jacket, and they were able to jump off the boat and swim with several boats guiding alongside.

For the food fight, we prepared bowls filled with some inexpensive foods like Jell-O and whipped cream. Each group gathered on the field near the beach, and we set ground rules and let the kids have a food fight before they jumped in the lake to clean up.

Swimming across the lake led to a conversation with the lifeguard and camp director to establish a swim test and safety protocols. By Friday, thirteen junior high kids had completed a forty-five-minute swim test and set off to swim across the lake with rowboats nearby. All the impossible adventures were truly possible with a bit of creativity and communication.

Doing the Impossible

The impossible doesn't need a qualifier or conditions attached to it to be considered impossible. It's what feels impossible for you. For some, it could be launching a podcast, writing a book, running a marathon, biking across the country, moving abroad, or completing a thru-hike trail. Regardless of what the impossible thing is, the intention for a boredom-busting adventure is to begin the simplest form of taking the next step forward as if you are already doing the impossible thing.

Just go for a hike. Just record yourself talking into your phone. Just write. Just go for a bike ride. Just do the thing without any expectation of quality or quantity. Just do the thing. The goal for this section is not to accomplish the impossible thing. It's simply to dream, to imagine, and break it into steps that you can do without feeling overwhelmed, without needing the right gear or getting into shape.

My kids often inspire me to do the impossible adventures. As I mentioned earlier, my youngest has been asking for a dirt bike for as long as he could talk. Today, I looked out the window, and he had snowboard boots, a full-face bike helmet, his dirt bike long-sleeved shirt, biking gloves, and skiing goggles on while riding his pedal bike in the backyard. He was doing the impossible thing. He was riding a dirt bike. There is nothing he is going to be able to do to progress toward a dirt bike at this stage. However, doing the impossible by way of creativity and imagination makes this a good example of shedding responsibilities, goals, and expectations and enjoying the potential experience.

Categories

Putting limits or boundaries around the possibilities can sometimes make the adventures more action-oriented. Last autumn, we started a tradition that has now become a fall family favorite known as Applefest. It's a weekend of unplugged camping when we focus on apple-based activities and foods. The only requirement is that we need to go apple picking the week before Applefest to have enough apples to cover all the activities.

Applefest also includes some complementary ingredients that pair well with apples, such as caramel, peanut butter, and cinnamon. Here is the list from Applefest this year:

- Making peanut butter play dough or simply adding cinnamon to store-bought Play-Doh
- Apple archery
- Apple tastings (rating on sweetness, color, and texture) or pairing with different cheese
- Hayride while sipping on apple cider or caramel apple suckers
- Apple pancakes with homemade cinnamon ice cream
- Grilled cheese with Granny Smith apple slices, bacon (Apples pair well with Gouda and Havarti cheese.) (*I should note this was much better than anyone expected!*)
- Pulled pork with apple BBQ sauce and roasted veggies
- Apple stamping
- Bobbing for apples
- Apple chucking contest

Categories can also be theme nights. Think in terms of countries, and create a theme night around one. Use a TV show or a color as a theme for a category. We have also thought about boundaries as physical boundaries, such as being restricted to a car while traveling long distances.

I don't think we have a lack of ideas. I think there is an abundance of ideas, and we get stuck trying to figure out which one to do. The good thing about adventure is that there are no wrong decisions. The goal is doing, not actually achieving any particular outcome. Hopefully, MAGIC can help wrap our arms around the possibilities and take action. The worst thing you can do is nothing!

Decision Fatigue

One of the many ways we get stuck is with decision fatigue. The human brain does better with fewer decisions. If we can put constraints around the possibilities, it increases the probability of action. Similarly, bunching, combining, or grouping activities leads to greater action and impact.

Key Takeaways

By using a little MAGIC, we add layers or filters on top of a previous activity creating a new memorable experience.

- We are more likely to take action if we reduce the number of overall options.
- Fewer decisions lead to a greater likelihood of action and impact.
- Using an existing perspective on a different opportunity helps us create new experiences. The acronym MAGIC is an example of this strategy
- MAGIC stands for Mismatched, Appearance, Generous, Impossible, and Categories
- What are you already good at that you can apply to family adventure?

Leading This Adventure

"The easiest thing is to react. The second easiest thing is to respond. But the hardest thing is to initiate."
—Seth Godin, *Tribes: We Need You to Lead Us*

The easy part is falling in line and doing as we are told or telling people what you think. That is what happens in the cheap seats. If you want to experience the beyond normal life, you must get in the arena. The hard part about designing a beyond normal life is that there are no clear lines.

Courage to Try

The dots might be scattered, and no one is telling you what the next moves are. For me, this is the step of courage, freedom, and abundance. While each of those are elements I crave, they also come with a daunting amount of fear, responsibility, and vulnerability. As Brené Brown says, "Joy is the most vulnerable emotion we experience, and if you cannot tolerate joy, what you do is you start dress rehearsing tragedy." I am eager to move forward in our adventurous lifestyle, but I know there is so much I have yet to figure out.

I am up for the challenge. This book isn't about me and my journey. It's never been about me. My purpose is to inspire families to *connect* through *adventure*. Let's bring back families being together. Let's allow kids to be kids. It's about allowing parents time and space to connect with their kids in simple and accessible ways. It's about finding meaning and joy in the struggle. It's about getting uncomfortable and stepping forward to take the first next step on this daring adventure. You can always make more money. Time and energy are depleting resources. This day will end. This week will never happen again. My son will never be six again.

I intend to stay grounded in this simple thought each day. These are the moments I want to remember. Sometimes, no matter what I am wading through, I need to take off my boots and play in the mud. Get dirty. Yes, at forty-something, it's still appropriate to play in the dirt. When you are on a glacier in Alaska, you wipe the glacier mud on your face!

Little Changes

The system is perfectly designed to get the results you are getting. If you don't like those results, you know what you need to do? Change something. Little changes, little actions are the epitome of progress in finding the path forward. No one is coming to rescue you. No one is going to magically do the laundry so you can go play. No one is going to tell you to get off the screen. No one is going to ask you to stop working so hard. That first step is completely yours to take.

Seasons of Life

Adventuring doesn't get easier the older you get. I caution others to be careful what you assign to the someday/maybe list. The list of somedays can be a death trap for ideas you don't believe in. If you want those experiences, you will take steps to make them happen. Some ideas do belong on the someday list.

There are seasons in our lives that will expire. I often need to remind myself that some ideas are okay for ten years from now. The only way the grass gets greener on the other side of the fence is when the owner is taking care of the grass. The grass is likely watered, trimmed, and potentially treated for weeds.

I am okay with a few weeds. I don't mind a yard with wildflowers and dandelions. My daughter once reminded my husband, who was expressing his disdain for the dandelions one summer, "Those aren't weeds, those are wishes!" I don't feel the need to prune and perfect each idea. Adventure as a family is a great practice in letting go of perfectionist tendencies.

Resilience Factor

Family systems theory shows the value of a shared experience has a lasting impact on a family's ability to bounce back from adversity. Each individual can have a unique and shared experience, even though the way they internalize or perceive the experience may be different. The simple act of sharing an experience makes it relatable and transferable for everyone involved. Adventure helps us practice sharing experiences together and overcoming challenges, strengthening overall family resiliency.

Research has shown that parents opt out of adventures because they are afraid their child will ask them a question and they won't know the answer. If that is you, know there are so many people and organizations available to support you without judgment. The impetus behind my podcast, *Ordinary Sherpa*, was to help families connect—connect as a family unit and connect to other families choosing a lifestyle of adventure no matter how big or small.

I wanted to connect people who are willing to share their own experiences and reach a hand back on the ladder to support someone else on the path. My adventure arena, and eventually my trusted adventure advisor circle, was developed by meeting others who have both similar and different experiences and circumstances but believe in our vision. They can offer insights and connections along the journey to help us prepare or inspire us through the struggle.

Leading this Adventure

The way to lead this adventure is to not go at it alone. *Ordinary Sherpa* can help you expedite and connect you to potential members of your adventure community. Long before I started writing this book, I began looking for my people. They are people in the arena and not simply sitting in the cheap seats. When I set out to build my own community, I began meeting with others, asking questions for my personal development.

I knew I needed to increase my exposure to what was possible. As people began joining my adventure community, they were excited for me; they wanted to see me succeed. You get to decide who is in your adventure community and which voices you listen to more intently. This life, this adventure, you will soon realize, is so much bigger than you. You will learn throughout the process about the power of being a Sherpa and the joy that comes from generosity and receivership.

Stir Up the Dream Pot

My boss often reminds me, "What got us here won't get us there. But what got us here, got us here." One of the greatest experiences was when a door closed in my life. It was the most beautiful no I ever received. It lit a fire of curiosity inside of me, leading me to see what the next chapter of my story will be.

My goal is to stir up the dream pot. Try not to worry about the details. Most of them are out of our control anyway. Be open to receiving an opportunity when it lands. The story you tell yourself about yourself is a shadow of your fate. We cannot protect ourselves from the human experience. We are designed for struggling. However, the margins of discomfort also offer fertile ground for growth.

Feedback Loop

Designing your life to be extraordinary is a constant feedback loop asking yourself a series of questions—practicing the action-feedback loop over and over again. To begin, define what you want. You get to choose what you will do differently today than you did yesterday. How are you allowing joy into your life? Who are the experienced adventurers you want to get in the arena with?

Designing a life is about constantly checking your compass and keeping joy as your North Star. How are you connecting and learning from others? The path forward is yours for the taking. It's up to you to take the first step. We'll be here to support you when you are ready.

Next Step

First of all, thank you for reading my book!

May I ask a quick favor? Will you take a moment to leave an honest review for this book on Amazon? Reviews are the BEST way to help others purchase the book. You can go to the link below and write your thoughts.

A written review is two to three sentences to help future readers determine if they should read the book. Some questions you might answer in the review are:

- Give insight into your demographic (ie As a working mom…) This helps readers determine how they are similar to you.
- What were one or two key things from the book you found helpful?
- How is this book different from other books you've read (in a similar genre)? You might even compare it to another book and explain how it differs.
- How did this book help you?
- What did you like about the writing style of the author? (Was it easy to read? Did it offer scientific research to support key points? Were the stories relatable?)

OrdinarySherpa.com/BeyondNormalReview

Acknowledgments

The adventure stories in this book wouldn't have come to life without some amazing people. My husband has supported every step of this process and has been a willing lifelong adventure partner. He keeps much of the work behind the scenes moving forward and I will forever be grateful for his willingness and commitment to keep our adventure stories alive. My three kids made my story more relevant for parents who crave adventure. They allowed me to keep going. Their curiosity and adventurous spirit inspire me every single day. I also need to thank my parents who got me on that first airplane, and never required me to stay grounded too long.

To the countless friends and family members who shaped a critical part of this story. To Grandpa Lange for introducing the love of the outdoors and to grandma for supporting all our shenanigans. Megan Draper, everyone needs a best friend who will not just support your crazy ideas, but volunteers to go along. To my marathon running crews, who supported the journey more than the finish. To extended family who offered countless destinations and crash-landing pads. To Kevin & Peg who modeled off-grid life way before it was trendy. To our foreign exchange students who opened my world and extended the borders of my community.

To experts who exposed me to the science offering data and relevance to my experiences. Such as neuroscientist, Richie Davidson; occupational therapist, Angela Hanscomb; the team at InteraWorks including CEO Laurie Oswold. To my boss and friend Marne Keller-Krikava for directly and indirectly mentoring and encouraging me to embrace both Mom and Executive roles. She was my pioneer in trusting both head and heart data and importance to both. There are many professional contacts turned friends from sharing authentically honest experiences of life. Thank you for being bold and continuing to write the story.

Ordinary Sherpa, the podcast and brand, was propelled into the market in 2020 thanks to the encouragement and support of two of my favorite podcasters, Jonathan Mendonsa and Brad Barrett of Choose FI. Through Jonathon's technical guidance and business expertise, and Brad's generous belief and sharing of my message. I have been the grateful recipient of many listeners. Choose FI inspired me to think about the long game differently. I commend their authentic leadership and inspiring voice in an often-noisy world.

Writing a book wasn't on the master plan of life. It came from a suggestion from several friends who either wrote books or supported authors. Through their generosity and inspiring words, I set off on this adventure. Skilled professionals like Kent Sanders who helped me establish the outline for this book and I went on to join his daily writer community. To Terry Staford, my editor, and also the voice that kept playing "write the book" over and over. Jennifer Harshman's team got me to the finish line. To several authors I now consider close friends, Rachel Richards and Andy Storch who shared countless tips to consider in getting this book into the world. I also want to acknowledge the individuals who volunteered to read my book before it was ready to publish and share feedback on the reader experience: Tracy Phillippi, Michael Grant, Jenya Lindstrom, Diane Nachel, Lynn Peters, Perry Gabbard, Daniela Toneva, Leslie Wheeling, Kelly Ryon, Julie McCarragher, Dawn Ruchala. Your feedback made this a much better book for readers today. For countless colleagues, friends and acquaintances who helped support the final stages getting this book into the universe.

Most importantly for you as a reader. I am so grateful you chose to spend your time reading this book. I hope this book inspires you to explore the depths of joy and recognize life is a thousand daring adventures, some without a summit experience. I hope parents feel empowered to get out and brave the wilderness with kids. I can't wait to hear all about your adventures!

About the Author

Heidi Dusek has earned the title of adventurous mom after over a decade of packing up kids and setting off on adventures near and far. She proudly wears the titles of Foundation Executive, Mom of 3, and wife to a DIY kind of guy and continues to live an intentional life challenging herself to not get too comfortable or align with the status quo. Some might describe her as a catalyst, disruptor and unshakeable optimist. Empathy and curiosity are critical threads in her fabric of an authentic and memorable life.

Her work is featured as the podcast host and founder of Ordinary Sherpa, an online community designed to inspire families to connect through simple and authentic adventure experiences. As an "ordinary" mom, she creates content to guide and support other families on their quest to live a more adventurous life.

Over the last 14 years of marriage, she and her husband, Brent, have traveled to over 40 states in an effort to support their 3 kids travel goals which include visiting all of the Major League Baseball stadiums, visiting all of the National Parks, and tasting the best small-batch homemade ice cream in all 50 states. Their strategies include a minimalist approach and budget using travel rewards, authentic connection with locals, and recently embarked on part-time RV life.

Heidi and Brent live in Northeast Wisconsin with their 3 kids and Weimaraner dog. They spend their time skiing, building igloos and making maple syrup and fill in the gaps the rest of the year hiking, mountain biking, and aim to spend as much time outdoors as possible. While they crave travel they also recognize the privilege and comforts of coming home.

Resources

All of the resources are available for free download at www.ordinarysherpa.com/beyondnormalbonus

1. Joy Audit: The Excel Spreadsheet is a tool to help you track your adventures and assign values to determine which experiences offer the greatest sources of joy.

2. Finders Seekers: The at home escape room that gave us a different type of national park experience.

3. Seasonal Adventure Lists: Each season we create a list of roughly twenty adventures to offer an intention for connection throughout the months ahead. We crowd source the adventure ideas getting us out of our comfort zone or encourage us to get curious. Included in the download are four seasonal adventure lists from our family.

4. Metrics of Thriving: is a downloadable tool to help redefine success. I adapted the Wheel of Life to align with our family values and establish what are key indicators of thriving in our life. Through reflection and experimentation, we continue to tweak these metrics and adapt to what makes us thrive.

5. Beginner's Guide to Travel Rewards: We have optimized our travel budget using travel rewards. This free download gives you our strategy and helps families navigate travel rewards. I also offer personal travel rewards strategy and coaching sessions.

6. Best Year Yet: This workshop offered by InteraWorks offers a framework that I used for lifestyle design. If you use my link you will receive a discounted rate.

Endnotes

1. TEDx Talks. (2019, December 12). "How Mindfulness Changes the Emotional Life of our Brains" | Richard J. Davidson | TEDxSanFrancisco [Video] https://www.youtube.com/watch?v=7CBfCW67xT8

2. Page, Oliver MD. (March 22, 2022). "How to Leave Your Comfort Zone and Enter Your Growth Zone." *Positive Psychology.* positivepsychology.com/comfort-zone

3. "Hedonic Treadmill" Wikipedia, Wikimedia Foundation, March 20, 2022, https://en.wikipedia.org/wiki/Hedonic_treadmill

4. Rowan Kelleher, Suzanne. July 28, 2019. Forbes:https://www.forbes.com/sites/suzannerowankelleher/2019/07/28/this-is-your-brain-on-travel/?sh=517766d92be6.

5. Fitzgerald, Meghan. "Why Kids' Vestibular Systems Need Exercise Every Day," Tinkergarten, April 9, 2021, tinkergarten.com/blog/a-hidden-sense-what-is-the-vestibular-sense

6. Flanders, Cait. *Adventures in Opting Out*, Little Brown Spark, 2020, Page 7.

7. "What are the 5 love languages? Discover Your Love Language" - The 5 Love Languages®. (n.d.) Retrieved April 8, 2022 from https://www.5lovelanguages.com/learn

8. Nurse Next Door (March 15, 2022). The value of shares experiences. Retrieved April 8, 2022, from https://www.nursenextdoor.com.au/blog/the-value-of-shared-experiences/

9. Lambert, Nathaniel M et al. (2012). A boost of positive affect: The perks of sharing positive experiences. Journal of Social and Personal Relationships, 30(1), 24-43. https://doi.org/10.1177%2F0265407512449400

10. Okura, Lynn. (October 18, 2013, Updated December 6, 2017). Brene Brown: "Joy is the Most Vulnerable Emotion We Experience." Huffpost. https://www.huffpost.com/entry/brene-brown-joy-numbing-oprah_n_4116520

11. TedX. (July 14, 2017). "Why you should define your fears instead of your goals" | Tim Ferris [Video]. YouTube. https://www.youtube.com/watch?v=5J6jAC6XxAI

12. Cherry, Kendra. "How the Fight-or-Flight Response Works," Verywell Mind, August 18, 2019. www.verywellmind.com/what-is-the-fight-or-flight-response-2795194

13. Mayo Clinic. (n.d) "Mindfulness Exercises," Mayo Clinic. Retrieved April 10, 2022 from https://www.mayoclinic.org/healthy-lifestyle/consumer-health/in-depth/mindfulness-exercises

14. Graff, Frank. "How Many Daily Decisions Do We Make," UNC TV | Science, February 7, 2018. science.unctv.org/content/reportersblog/choices

15. Fields Millburn, Joshua and Nicodemus, Ryan. "Minimalism: AN Elevator Pitch," The Minimalists. https://www.theminimalists.com/pitch/

16. McKee, Spencer, "The Cost of a Family Ski Trip to Colorado," Out There Colorado, October 12, 2017. www.outtherecolorado.com/category/breckenridge/the-cost-of-a-family-ski-trip-to-colorado/article_3b4f7ad1-50ee-5b8f-b293-d261b5bdc7f4.html

17. "Picky Eaters and What to Do" CDC Nutrition, updated December 17, 2020 https://www.cdc.gov/nutrition/infantandtoddlernutrition/foods-and-drinks/picky-eaters.html Accessed February 6, 2022.

18. James, Ed, et al. Be More Kid. Wiley, 2021, Page 19.

19. Kepnes, Matt. Ten Years a Nomad. St. Martin's Press, 2019, page 76-77.

20. "Book Summary: Tribes by Seth Godin" Sam Thomas Davies. Published July 19, 2021, https://www.samuelthomasdavies.com/book-summaries/ business/tribes   Accessed April 10,2022.

21. KatieMae. "Are You in a Circle or in a Cage?" Medium. Published June 28, 2019 https://medium.com/@katiemaeonline/are-you-in-a-circle-orin- a-cage-460445dd46e0. Accessed April 10, 2022.

22. Johnsrud, Jillian. Fire the Haters. 2021. Page 73.

23. Jannazzo, Eric S. "You are Good Enough" Psychology Today, Published March 2, 2021.   https://www.psychologytoday.com/us/articles/202103/you-are-good-enough. Accessed April 9, 2022.

24. Madore, Kevin P, and Anthony D Wagner. "Multicosts of Multitasking." Cerebrum : the Dana Forum on Brain Science, The Dana Foundation, 1 Apr. 2019, https://www.ncbi.nlm.nih.gov/pmc/articles/PMC7075496/.

25. Brown, Brené. Dare to Lead: Brave Work, Tough Conversations, Whole Hearts. New York: Random House Large Print, 2019.

26. Brodrick, Melissa. "The Heart and Science of Kindness." Harvard Health, 18 Apr. 2019, https://www.health.harvard.edu/blog/the-heart-and-science-of-kindness-2019041816447.

27. "Study: Volunteering Is Good for Your Health." News, 16 June 2020,   https://www.hsph.harvard.edu/news/hsph-in-the-news/study-volunteering-is-good-for-your-health/#:~:text=Older%2520adults%2520who%2520volunteer%2520for,Chan%2520School%2520of%2520Public%2520Health.

28. Okura, Lynn. "The Most Vulnerable Emotion We Experience." HuffPost, HuffPost, 7 Dec. 2017, https://www.huffpost.com/entry/brene-brown-joy-numbing-oprah_n_4116520.